pulling my selves together

…an extremely moving work,
written with a candour rarely found.
KEVIN GUY
Journal for the National Council of Psychotherapists

PULLING MY SELVES TOGETHER

Re-inventing Reality & Achieving Wholeness

DILYS GATER

ANECDOTES
PUBLISHING

LAP

Don

First published in 2000 as
PULLING MY SELVES TOGETHER:
Overcoming Dissociative Personality Disorder

This new expanded edition published in 2004 by:
Anecdotes
38 Grosvenor Street
Leek, Staffordshire
ST13 5NA

Paperback ISBN: 1 898670 08 0

British Library Cataloguing in Publication Data
A Catalogue record of this book is available from the British Library

Printed by:
The Basingstoke Press
Digital House
The Lodden Centre
Wade Road
Basingstoke
Hants, RG24 8QW

Cover picture: Mark Campbell
Cover design: Steve Bishop, Origin8

To Peggy Poole ('Charlotte'), writer and friend,
To Graham F. Humphreys ('D'),
To Judith Barratt ('Lara'), my daughter,
With thanks and love.

Also dedicated with gratitude to Mum and Dad.
And to all who recognise themselves in these pages.
We are never as alone as we think.

CONTENTS

INTRODUCTION

As a practising psychic, medium and healer, I am consulted by hundreds of people a year. I have worked as a psychic counsellor for over ten years throughout London and the South of England, as well as during the last few years in the Midlands where I now live. I write books about my work, lecture and teach.

But this was not always the case since I came to awareness of my psychic potential comparatively late in life after years marked by 'breakdowns', emotional instability and the suspicion that I was not merely ill but possibly 'mad' – whatever that entailed. Even when psychic awareness came, the road to self-discovery and the realisation of my own true reality – which brought the ability to begin bringing the fragments of a disturbed existence together – was not easy.

It was in 1987 when I was forty-three, a professional writer and author of over seventy books, that I wrote this account of my struggle to overcome the personality disorder and unspecified, but incapacitating illness that had plagued me throughout my adult life. I had undergone years of treatment including psychiatric counselling, ECT (Electro Convulsive Therapy), spells as an in- as well as out-patient in at least four different psychiatric hospitals and heavy doses of prescribed drugs including Valium, to which I became addicted.

I had never quite been told I was 'mad' – but it was obvious that I could not honestly be described as 'sane' either! And I had reached a point where I felt I could go no further, that I had to re-evaluate my whole existence, my sense of self and my sense of reality. In desperation, unable to trust doctors or psychiatrists – or indeed trust anyone to help me –

I began the long and tortuous journey into the depths of my own heart and mind to try and find the answers there that I so desperately sought.

With the support of 'Charlotte', a long-standing friend in Cheshire who was also a writer, and 'D.', the man with whom I lived in London at that time, I spent eight weeks undergoing what turned out to be the most gruelling form of self-analysis, returning to the dark areas of my childhood and examining the fears, traumas and patterns of behaviour that had tormented me for so long. Not until years later, when I had also been able to appreciate and acknowledge that much of my supposed 'madness' had been caused by ignorance of my 'second-sightedness' and intense psychic gifts – sternly repressed by all around me and unsuspected by myself – did I realise my journey had also been the start of the spiritual pilgrimage that still continues.

Because it helped (as it often does in difficult situations) to externalise the problem, treat it as though it belonged to someone else and thus achieve some kind of detachment, I wrote the account under another name, that of 'Tanya Bruce'. And so this is Tanya's 'Book', her story. Her first-hand account of how she went back to the source of her whole existence, her whole perception of reality, and tried to re-establish herself and her relationship with the world – indeed, the worlds – around her in a truer light. It was written from moment to moment, as a daily record of her thoughts and feelings, her honest and unabridged reporting of everything that occurred as her mental journey progressed. In the most realistic sense this was a live recording, since neither she nor any of the two people who knew what she was doing, had the faintest clue what to expect.

Charlotte explained later:

'Having written the early chapters and come to a point where she felt she could go no further without another voice, Tanya asked me to co-operate with her over this book. I had not, as we admitted to each other later, the slightest idea of what would be involved… but I did believe, after reading the earlier part of her manuscript, that the exercise seemed a worthwhile one, though I doubted whether anything I said or thought could be of much help.

'Neither of us knew what would happen. Writing of the sort of life Tanya has led could never, I realised, be easy, but we both felt that our route, however tortuous, would have recognisable landmarks. We did not expect to journey into unmapped areas; mapped, no doubt, somewhere, but certainly not for me, nor for Tanya.'

Charlotte and D. admitted afterwards that each had secretly wondered whether Tanya would actually survive the 'terrible journey'. And she had the same fear herself, as she wrote later when she had been working for some years as a psychic counsellor and healer:

'While I was struggling with my anger and hate, typing through the tearful pages of the Book, I could not possible have envisaged that I would ever achieve anything like the detachment and balance necessary to be able to help anyone. I was aware that I might be helping by example, as it were, with my experiences as a sort of cautionary tale so that others might benefit from the results I found in the end – if I found any. But it was possible, and I was only too aware of this myself at the time, that my mind would give up completely and I would lose all touch with reality.'

I was the actual physical person who lived through the learning experiences recorded in this book. I was the one who wrote them down. Yet I am not Tanya, and Tanya is not me. She was the person I was then, the woman who brought me to the realisation of my self and the fact that I could acknowledge and be proud of that self, and accept after years of struggling that the 'I' that I am is the 'I' I was meant to be. Her name appears as the author of this work rather than my own because I want to step aside and let her tell her story in her own words. For these were the words and feelings, the fears and strivings of the moment, as it was when the battle was raging, as things were at that time.

I cannot help feeling empathy as I look back now at my younger self struggling so painfully with her problems, perceptions and terrors. But I have moved on and am, I hope, not only older but wiser, feeling no need to dwell on the past. I might also add here that it is some years since I smoked or took any drugs at all on a regular basis.

I have studied and read widely concerning the conditions I appeared to encounter during my years of 'illness' – that 'illness' that was never actually identified by any doctor or psychiatrist – and notes enlarging on various aspects of the subject of healing and 'wholeness' appear at the end of the book. What eventually brought me peace and a sense of unity was the realisation that every part of the self – on whatever level – must be recognised and integrated. The process of integration is not finite either but is in a continual state of balance and it is the maintaining of that balance which matters rather than conformity to any rigid pattern. Peace and happiness are not goals to achieve but states of mind where the scenery is continually changing.

This is the theme of this book. It is the record of one person's quest but hopefully it will encourage others to pursue their own search and make their own journey, however tortuous or difficult. The great spiritual journeys of all our lives have to be made in this way, blindfolded, in fear and in faith. And it is only by summoning the courage to try and make them that we are able to grow in maturity and stature, to discover our true potential and take the place intended for us in the world – in the process achieving the peace and sense of wholeness within ourselves that so many of us vainly long for.

The events as they are described in this volume covered some nine weeks of concentrated mental effort. Tanya's original early chapters, involving her groping back to the traumas of her childhood and trying to face them, were too painfully personal and subjective to be useful here, and have not been included. Any important points were touched on later either in her own reflections or her conversations with Charlotte. What is particularly relevant however, is her account of the 'Double Bind' syndrome as she understood and recorded it, and this is included in her own words in the Appendix.

We begin her book after she had made contact with Charlotte and asked for her friend's assistance, when as we will see, she was then able to begin moving forward. *Tanya's Book* forms the first part of this volume and it came to an involuntary end when, mentally exhausted and physically ill from the struggle, she was nevertheless able to feel she had broken the chains of her past and held the key to the future. Empty of all except the sensation of having been refined and re-focussed as a new and more truthful self, she made what she thought was to be the final entry in her chronicle of her journey through the dark and the battles with her demons.

'The Book' was finished. It was all over. Or was it?

This might have seemed the end – and indeed, to the three participants, it did hopefully appear so. As a writer though, Tanya could not stop writing and with no idea of what she could expect or how she would cope, she began the next day to note down what occurred, keeping a record of her further progress in a diary.

Tanya's Diary (originally published separately) forms the second half of this book. It illustrates that it is not the great decisions, the huge cataclysmic battles that are often the hardest to fight in our everyday lives. The application of our hard-won wisdom, the attempts to live honestly, as best we can, to the limit of our capabilities at all times, without deluding ourselves, in the face of the trials and temptations, the million little pin-pricks of mundane living, can cost us far more. For as Tanya soon discovered, one great battle is not the end. It may even be only the beginning. The struggle for truth and wholeness goes on unceasingly.

But as she wrote later, in retrospect:

'Somehow I felt throughout the whole terrible experience a strange sense of certainty, a conviction that I was doing what I had to do, and going the way it was necessary for me to go. I did not understand why, yet I felt that matters were out of my hands, that I was following a path ordained. Later it seemed the experience had been necessary, the suffering and torment some sort of initiation to prepare me for what was to come. For out of the darkness, in the end, was to spill the most priceless treasure, far beyond anything I could have anticipated or even imagined – jewels of wisdom, pearls of understanding.'

I consider myself privileged to have undergone the experiences I have known and been able to learn from them and grow through them. The terrors that Tanya struggled so hard to overcome have faded, since true strength is not the absence of fear but the ability to face and confront it. There is no 'right way' but an honest resolve to do what seems best at any given time, to the best of one's ability, in trust that somehow, one will cope. Faith in a higher power – whether God, Spirit or some other perceived source of strength and enlightenment – comes naturally when one is able to humbly accept one's own human limitations.

This record is for all who have ever struggled as I did, to 'reinvent' themselves truthfully, rebuild their lives after dissociative trauma, of whatever kind, or simply to discover a sense of integrity and wholeness both within and without. I hope there will be something in it that will help you.

Dilys Gater 2004

FOREWORD
by Dr Marie Campkin

This is the story of a woman's struggle towards recovery from long-term mental illness. The title aptly conveys the essence of the writer's problem – a personality so fragmented by painful early experience that she had spent her life being possessed and driven in turn by one or other of its conflicting aspects.

She had gained little benefit from conventional medical treatment over many years. Eventually she used her experience as a writer, and the tools of her trade – curiosity, humour and a capacity for detached observation – to achieve a breakthrough. She subjected herself – or her selves – to a period of the most intense self-examination and exploration, pouring all her memories, emotions and thoughts into writing until at last some understanding and resolution began to emerge from the melting-pot.

Immediately afterwards she began a diary chronicling the course of her recovery. Having identified and named – or rather, numbered – the three chief characters in her internal drama, she began the task of trying to integrate them into a functioning whole person; not rejecting, denying or favouring one against another but treating them all with equal respect, affection and acceptance.

This book is her account of that difficult, painful but ultimately triumphant process. It covers only a period of weeks, but the years which have elapsed since these events took place have confirmed the significance and durability of the changes that came about as a result. And though this is a personal account of an individual's unique experience, many people reading it will find themselves identifying with aspects of it.

Those who have never suffered any form of mental distress may gain some understanding of their many fellow-beings who have. Even more will those who have suffered illness – no matter what the precise label attached to their disorder – recognise familiar feelings; incomprehension, self-disgust and despair, but also insight, acceptance, relief and hope for a better future. And those who deal professionally with mentally disturbed people could also learn something of what it feels like at the other end of the therapy.

Dr Campkin is a London GP.

Freedom is a heavy load, a great and strange burden for the spirit to undertake. It is not easy. It is not a gift given, but a choice made, and the choice may be a hard one. The road goes upward towards the light, but the laden traveller may never reach the end of it.

The Tombs of Atuan
URSULA LE GUIN

We are, I know not how, double in ourselves, which is the cause that what we believe we do not believe, and cannot disengage ourselves from what we condemn.

Of glory – Essays
MONTAIGNE

Whatever you may be sure of, be sure of this: that you are dreadfully like other people.

JAMES RUSSELL LOWELL

There is no escape.
Down the long avenues of sleep
                    lies the awaking:
Seek solace in a flower –
                    the petals perish:
Ascend the steepest hill
                    descent must follow:
Accelerate along the road –
                    the end comes sooner.

There is no escape.
Eschew the chase
stand and study the pursuer
and find it is –
                    yourself.

Peggy Poole

                              *

Hold

And when the blackness comes
hold
while the heart sleeps,
while you lose shape,
hold.
It is the wilderness
and there are two ways out –
hold
do not go that way,
full and broken by knowledge –
hold still and soft
as a low mist. If the cat comes
don't spit back. Hold for the coming
of the cool wind, morning
and the heart opening slow as a reluctant tulip
in a cold April.

Diana Hendry (with kind permission)

TANYA'S BOOK

1
UNTO THE UNKNOWN

Ten past five in the morning. Still dark. Early traffic beginning to break the stillness – one lone car passing, then another. Silence again. I'm sitting with the lights on, drinking tea and smoking. Can't sleep. I'm a traveller too, I've been going down, down into what must be the deepest caverns of my mind. You couldn't go on for long at this level of thought and I don't know whether what I'm doing is wise, or even safe. Maybe I might become caught in the depths and never be able to return but I feel I've got to risk it if this manuscript is to have any real meaning at all.

When I started to write the first pages, to actually try and put my innermost self down into words, it must have been because the right time had come to make this attempt, because I'd reached the end of the road so far as being able to cope in any normal sort of manner was concerned. Couldn't live, couldn't die. Trusted no-one, nothing, knew the utter futility of screams, tears, expectations of any sort of help, existed in a miasma of pain and increasing sense of detachment from reality. No hope left. Nothing is there. Nothing matters.

I'd thought of suicide – thought of running – I did neither this time. And when even those two last desperate standbys I have always viewed as my final line of defence – escape – in the past had ceased to hold any prospect of freeing me from the grinding ache of having to try and make a token show of actually being a creature whose heart was still beating, maybe then I felt subconsciously that by trying to write it all down I'd find something to cling into, some way back.

I could never have written this book before, at any time in my life. And all through the pages I have been feeling my way. It's been like making a journey blindfolded, into uncharted territory. I still don't know where I am going, whether there will be an end to my journey, or even whether the end will be worse than it was at the beginning, but I have no choice. I have to go on because there's nothing for me if I go back.

In the beginning I thought I knew myself well, I even thought I had perhaps been able to put my life into some sort of pattern after all the thinking and wondering and struggling to come to terms over the last forty-odd years. I suppose I imagined the end product would be a kind of record, a picture of the real me that I've tried so hard to keep hidden, that I've never let anyone see, not to any meaningful degree. It hasn't worked out like that. I've blundered about – I'm still blundering about – and the actual working out of my thoughts is showing me that my knowledge of myself is pitiful, superficial. Even at this stage, I can see when I look back at the early pages that I've already travelled an unbelievable distance from when I wrote them, under the impression I was recording my most basic, fundamental feelings and beliefs.

One might think I must have been aware of the significant patterns – methods of behaviour – before but this is not so. I didn't even start to identify incidents and traits as having any connection with each other until I came to describe them in these pages. It's as if I have a handful of jigsaw pieces, every one of which I can see separately, without being able to fit them together to make a picture. And even when I manage to grasp one picture, I travel deeper into my mind and see that picture is only another jigsaw piece in a more complex picture. It's like opening up a series of Chinese boxes, one inside the other, endlessly, or a set of Russian dolls.

I suppose this is how self-knowledge is acquired, not in one blinding flash but in a long and painful seeking out and acceptance of first a simple truth, which might seem the answer but is only part of an even wider truth, and so on.

The thing that amazes me is that through all the events of my life there have been clues, signposts that now appear so obvious I can't understand why I did not see their significance before. Why has it taken me forty-three years to be able to gain even the small amount of insight that writing this book is giving me? I have chronicled the disasters I've detailed in these early pages to so many doctors and psychiatrists that I am sick of repeating the story, I've pleaded from the depths of misery and despair for assistance to 'sort myself out'. Yet nowhere, in all my listening, my reading, my searching, have I found one voice that could tell me anything to guide me in the right direction, help me to make sense of the jumbled fragments of my past.

Is it left to every one of us to make such a painful journey into the depths of our souls, in order to try and ease the agony of having to try and progress from our birth to our death? Do 'normal' people have to do this? Or is it something that is part of my illness, my sickness, my own individual and personal problems?

I am stumbling about in the dark. The only thing I am sure of is that in the depths of my consciousness, I have touched off through the writing of this book, the most traumatic crisis of my life. I will never be the same again. It is shattering, mind-blowing. But since I cannot go back I have to carry on, though how far, or what I will discover – if anything – before I reach some sort of end – if there is an end – I can't tell.

In the past I have become familiar with most of the usual forms of treatment meted out by doctors and in hospitals for depression and whatever else I suffer from – though I can of course only describe these treatments from the point of view of an observant and enquiring sufferer. What I was given most often – presumably because the immediate necessity in a case of extreme depression, agitation or distress is to ease the pain and remove some of the tension and stress from the patient – was drugs

If a GP, harassed, over-worked, is faced with a very distressed person who comes back time and time again but who seems to be able to function reasonably well on an everyday basis and keep going somehow, I imagine there is really little else he/she can do except prescribe a tranquilliser or an anti-depressant, a sleeping tablet or a muscle relaxant (with all of which I am familiar) and add a few bracing words to help the patient on his/her way. I have taken various drugs – as prescribed – in varying dosages ever since I was twenty-one. Maybe I will have to rely to a certain extent on drugs for the rest of my life.

When times have been particularly bad I have leaned far more heavily on drugs than is wise to do. In the most terrible years I was taking heavy doses of several other drugs each day as well as Valium, the strength of which crept up as I returned more and more upset to my doctor. It went from 2mg to 10mg and since the prescribed number of tablets quite often had no effect I took them in larger and larger amounts, often six or eight 10mg tablets in twenty-four hours, sometimes more. And even those terrific doses didn't seem to work. I still couldn't sleep, I couldn't rest, I couldn't relax, the manic energy would not leave me. I was quite literally exhausted to my very bones, but unable to stop.

When a certain amount of the stress had been removed, when I was a little more steady, I decided to break my dependence on drugs, starting with the Valium. I simply stopped taking it overnight. I'd got to get a grip on myself, I thought.

What followed was horrific. I began to experience all the symptoms of withdrawal without realising what they were. I had been an addict, a drug addict without knowing it, and (since I had moved home) I hadn't consulted my new doctor about weaning myself from the Valium, simply decided not to take them any more, to try and cope without. As I already suffered from so many symptoms of chronic stress, however, I regarded all the effects of withdrawal as just a few more inexplicable little burdens I had to shoulder, and plodded on doggedly. It was only when a friend – my one close friend except for Charlotte, even though she now lived miles from me – suggested tentatively that maybe the symptoms I mentioned to her had something to do with my dropping the Valium that D., concerned, brought home some literature on drug abuse and we looked up the possibility.

It was all there, of course. I cannot remember all the symptoms I had now but one medical book describes the withdrawal symptoms from Valium as 'convulsions, tremors, abdominal and muscle cramps, and sweating'. I had others too – extreme anxiety, vertigo, blurring of vision, exhaustion for example, and one I recall particularly, a terrible crawling sensation of the skin.

At the time, I was not concerned with making notes about what I was feeling and I had already been experiencing the symptoms for some time before we realised what was causing them. When I did consult my doctor and she suggested that I should try to alleviate them by taking smaller doses of Valium before cutting them out altogether, I thought that would only prolong the agony. I could stand it if D. could put up with me, I decided, and carried on somehow until after several months the worst of the symptoms must have worn off: I was too busy trying to cope with the usual depression and tension to make much of them. It was at this point that my husband, with whom I was still on caring and affectionate terms though I had not been able to continue living with him, suddenly, shockingly and most unexpectedly died of a heart attack. So I had the grief and pain of his death to cope with as well.

*

Until I tried to cut my wrists and went into hospital for the first time at twenty-two, I had no treatment at all since nobody realised there was anything wrong with me. I didn't realise it myself. I had always blamed myself, presuming that if things seemed difficult to cope with it was because of some deficiency in me, and that it was up to me to try harder and do better.

In the hospital I was given drugs for the first time, and also learned of what I think is probably the most helpful and beneficial treatment for any sufferer – being given the opportunity to talk about your problems to an informed listener. Cliché though it may be, there is nothing that brings more relief when you are distressed or disturbed – or even sunk in depression – than being able to communicate your feelings to another person. The whole theory of psychoanalysis is based on communication, and even phrases like 'get it off your chest' express a fundamental truth. And yet I feel many people are completely unaware of the pitfalls, the dangers and complexities – even the fallacies – inherent in turning to a friend, or even a doctor or psychiatrist for help.

Most people suffering from emotional or mental imbalance and distress will plead desperately for help yet however many doctors they go to, however many psychiatrists they consult in their frantic search, basically, deep down, they do not really want to be 'cured'. They will dig their toes in, they will argue with their psychiatrist and turn their sessions of therapy into a battle of wills. I have seen this in the eyes of people suffering from depression, the challenge, the barrier put up. So you think you can cure me, do you? Go right ahead, in your knowledge and your wisdom, bring in the big guns, do all you can, but if you succeed in getting to me it will be over my dead body. Go on, I dare you!

This may seem a ridiculous statement to make when the sufferers are so very obviously in great need, when they will agree to try one method of treatment after another in order to alleviate their suffering. But to them, their depression, their suffering and pain is only the defence they have put up unconsciously in order to protect themselves from deeper hurts which are the basic root of their trouble and which they find it impossible to face up to and try to deal with. If their suffering is taken away, stripped from them, they will have nothing between them and the terrible root of their problems, a prospect so horrifying to contemplate that they will go through anything, even a suicide attempt, rather than accept it.

Speaking for myself, I am no different to other suffers in this respect. I didn't want to be cured – I don't know that I want to be cured even now. But looking back to the earlier part of this manuscript I can see that what I was doing (completely unconsciously, thinking I was putting down my deepest thoughts and emotions and I have come a long way since I started to write) was what all patients do in the early stages of therapy. Thresh around blindly trying to communicate their pain and at the same time assert that they have a right to remain just as they are.

This is what it's like, I was saying, this is how I am, why shouldn't I be like this, why can't people accept me in my awful flawed state? I want you all to love me whether I'm flawed or not, why can't you do that?

What the sufferers want – what they imagine they want – from their friends or their psychiatrist is some sort of recognition of their suffering, and a lot of sympathy because their lot is so hard, their life is so tragic, they have such a difficult row to hoe. I must have written this myself somewhere in those early pages – that wail of 'Why me? Why should this have happened to me? The least people can do is acknowledge that I'm having a terrible time – I mean, under all this stiff-upper-lip and small brave smile, I'm really being awfully courageous about everything, aren't I? I do deserve to be congratulated – it isn't easy, no-one can possibly understand the effort I put into keeping going. If anyone else was trying so hard they'd get a medal for it, so why can't I have a bit of credit for all this suffering I'm going through so nobly? Why won't people notice how badly I hurt, why won't they tell me how wonderful I am to make so little fuss about it? I mean, it's bloody hard on me and I'm really doing ever so well.'

Oh yes, even when I thought I was writing something stirring and challenging in those early chapters, something that would provoke – perhaps – serious comment, I can see now, after the week of crisis I've gone through talking to Charlotte that what I was really expressing was my own self-pity, my conviction that my sufferings ought to be recognised and praised and rewarded. My viewpoints have altered drastically in these last few days, when Charlotte and I have spent hours communicating on the very deepest level. I've gone into the depths of myself, too frightened to take such an immense step alone, needing her no-nonsense, tough tenderness to keep me steady, her reassurance that I hadn't already gone over the edge into insanity. I'm not even the same person I was when I wrote the first part of this book and I'm still unbelievably unsure of myself, knowing I have a long way left to go even though I've come so far so fast.

I'm not even certain of where I am at this moment, but it's a lot further forward than pouring out the grief and confusion, anguish and anger that must have been churning inside me, piling up like water behind a dam, in my forty-three years of living. Without any cracks of thunder, flourish of trumpets, quivering of the earth's crust, something cataclysmic has happened to Tanya Bruce. It hasn't affected the world, outwardly I have not changed, none of the people I might pass in the street will ever know that in the course of five – six – days talking long into the night with Charlotte, the dam finally burst within me and all the struggling, the pain, the despair, the misery of the past, the bewilderment, the anger, the hopelessness, came crashing over me in surge after surge, choking me and drowning me, sweeping me along in the murky waters, spinning me in whirlpools, throwing me up again, tossing me like a doll with the weight of power behind it.

I am still gasping, unsure of myself as the tumult begins to recede. I said to Charlotte that it must have been just as traumatic for her to be there witnessing what I was suffering, what was happening to me, and that I had not intended to involve her in all that emerged after she read the early part of my manuscript and wanted to talk me through some more of it, help me to carry on.

'I had no idea what was going to happen. I didn't expect anything like this,' I told her.

'I don't think either of us did,' she said.

*

Until I started writing this book, until I reached the point where I found it too painful to go any further alone and asked Charlotte to help me continue if she thought it was worth finishing – though as I have mentioned, I had no idea at all of how it would actually proceed once we began to talk – I suppose what I imagined I wanted was what most 'mentally ill' people are unconsciously looking for in their desperation and their pain. Recognition of my suffering, sympathy, and the right to exist as a mute and hideous mental cripple.

I too must have defied the doctors and the psychiatrists through years of searching for the 'cure' I couldn't face. But we all have to create our own salvation. Now I can see that the same psychiatrists who (as I bitterly complained in the early pages) 'told me nothing' did in fact tell me quite a lot. In the manner of the sufferers I have described, though, I shut my ears. I refused to listen. I didn't want to know.

One cannot blame a sufferer for doing this, for fighting against well-meant efforts to give them the help they are so urgently requesting. For while depression and inability to cope are extremely painful and can cripple and paralyse, becoming unbearable to live with, the 'talking treatment' – psychoanalysis – is not only even more traumatic, it is utterly terrifying. It involves feelings, experiences that are entirely alien and just as death is frightening because it is the 'great unknown', so to most people the process of descending into the deep recesses of their minds is equally such a journey into the unknown. The patient is not asking for such probing into dark and unfamiliar worlds, for confrontations with his soul – it would be too horrifying, too stark. The mind must be handled gently, and can only accept what it is able to take, which varies with every individual.

Maybe because I am a writer to whom the workings of the mind are my raw material, it was easier when I felt I was alienated from the world, drifting into myself since there was nothing familiar left to hold onto, for me to try and go into the dark. I have lived a lot of my life with consciousness of the unknown, perhaps to me it is not so utterly terrifying as the known, the reality. Though even so far as I have managed to travel has not been easy.

In the early pages I suppose I followed the pattern of psychoanalysis without realising it. I regressed back into remembered pain, suffering, guilt, shame, fear. It was hard to chronicle the incidents of the past, as the feelings I had suffered when they occurred came back and I had to live through them when I was writing. Many times I had to stop because I had become too depressed, or because I was unbearably angry, outraged, bewildered and the emotions beat unmercifully at me to be let out, to find expression I was unable to give them. By the time I had written two or three chapters I had moved on a little in my self-imposed 'therapy'. The present was beginning to intrude onto the past and I was starting to include my present feelings, describing them if not actually as they occurred, then immediately afterwards, when I was able to write them down.

The pain did not ease at this point, it increased, until I knew I couldn't cope any more without some sort of help and that was when I turned to Charlotte. Her acceptance, her wisdom, her new viewpoints, her comments – all of these gave me the strength to step into the maelstrom, the abyss – though I did it without my own volition. Now I am in the aftermath, but the grinding, gnawing agony of living has eased a little. I am not so depressed. I am not so despairing. I am able to move forward.

*

The probable reaction of any decent human being, when confronted by someone in the depths of misery who is quite obviously suffering, will be to want to sympathise with them. But strange to say, the sympathy the sufferer thinks he craves will provoke not a relief from his pain but a feeling of contempt for those who offer it. The suffering generally despise people who sympathise with them and sympathy may not be the virtue it is made out to be. It can be one of the most useless and dangerous of all expressions of emotion.

The definition of 'sympathy' in my dictionary is: 'Participation in feeling (capacity for) being affected similarly to another by his sensations etc., compassion (for).' And whole it is certainly necessary to possess an ability to understand and share another person's sensations so far as this is possible, participation in them – certainly in my own case – has proved itself over and over again to be worth absolutely nothing at all, of no benefit to anyone, doing damage and harm. Compassion is a different matter. I sense Charlotte's compassion – D.'s compassion – but if either of them were to express their compassion for me in a conventionally sympathetic manner I know I would turn from them immediately, cut myself off.

All the characteristics of what we commonly call 'sympathy', the gentle, understanding voice, the patient attitude, the agreement with complaints that may be made – 'Yes, it must be absolutely terrible for you, I know exactly how you feel, it's awful, I really do sympathise' – these do nothing but drive the unfortunate sufferer to screaming pitch. If you are miserable it does no good, it is no help, if everyone else decides that because they are sympathetic and want to share your misery, they will sit down and howl with you. Even the gentle tone of understanding so often used towards the less fortunate who have more problems than we have ourselves, is likely to provoke nothing more than for the less fortunate to turn round and snap viciously: 'For God's sake, stop being so bloody patronising'. If they are forced by circumstances to suffer this sort of 'sympathy' in silence, their resentment will build up unbearably.

Perhaps it's a question of communication. Unfortunately, we rarely know what we are saying, we only know what we are trying to say. Concern, compassion, if expressed as 'sympathy', will almost always be fiercely rejected or violently resented. And the unexpectedness of such a negative, even aggressive reaction when one is genuinely and spontaneously trying to help can be upsetting and hurtful. There are misunderstandings, frustrations on all sides.

If someone says 'I know exactly how you must feel', indicating thereby that they are prepared to feel that way too in order to express their sympathy, they are denying the sufferer the right to cope with his bad feelings himself. They are also adding to his burden by unconsciously creating the need for him to cope with having to express gratitude, free himself from an obligation to his helper.

The most sensible way of dealing with someone shaken with misery and despair is to provide them with something to mop up their tears themselves, and go quietly about the ordinary business of living in a matter-of-fact manner. A cup of tea handed over to the trembling wreck without comment or condescension will be of far more help to them than all the verbal gushings of concern in the world, however kindly meant.

It's not easy to watch someone else suffering and do nothing except try to ease their pain in small, practical ways. The impulse is to gather them up, cradle them, protect them, share their hurt. But no-one can live another person's life, no-one can go through his suffering for him. And though the Bible says: 'Bear ye one another's burdens' this cannot be done in the sense in which most people interpret it, since it is impossible to bear the burden another individual must carry. Help can – and indeed, most certainly should – be given, but even the most desperately sick person is still a human being in his or her own right, and to deny them that right, the right to at least try in their small, quavering, uncertain, trembling way to find the minimum of self-control, self-respect, ability to cope as best they can, is to damage and wound to a shocking degree.

It is the cruellest and most arrogant action anyone can take against someone else. You might as well kill them off – shoot them – for you are passing exactly this same judgement on them by smothering them with 'sympathy' and attempting to assume their suffering. In effect you are saying: 'This person is not competent, he doesn't understand how to go about living. I know better, so I will do it and live for him.'

Such well-meant interference in another's life – his very personal, private, rightful, unique existence – is the equivalent of mental murder. So is it any wonder that the unstable, the feeble and their like, can hate and loathe and despise their killers who, in the name of love, of duty, of 'sympathy', often perform inexorable and unforgivable slaughters through every moment of every hour of every day?

2
THE FURY FACTOR

It isn't just anger, it's rage, fury, boiling and seething, shaking me, every inch of me, inside and out. Murderous, vitriolic. I am helpless, at a standstill, I'm aware of nothing except this monumental living ache of feeling crashing painfully and impotently at the furthest extremities of my mind and my body. Not only fury but hate as well, so fierce, so powerful that it's like being held upright by the force that's hurtling from one part of me to the other, blindly seeking escape, in the eye of a whirlwind. If it should go away suddenly, this minute, I'd fall, I couldn't stand. It's driving me, driving me so that my mind is racing ahead of time. The whole world outside seems to have slowed down, I have passed it, I'm way out in front somewhere.

This is what I've experienced so many times before, but I didn't see then that it was anger, rage, hate, I didn't recognise it. The trembling, the shaking, the gasping to breathe, the sickness, the nausea inside. No way out, turning back on itself, turning inwards destroying me as it goes, churning me up, reducing me to nothing. A waste land, laid low, just spindly twigs left of the trees, everything flattened. Oh God how I hate. Hate, hate, hate, hate, hate. Hurling my fury into a void, I cannot hurt or hit out, the void is myself, I am trapped within my own dumbness.

Did my mother hate like this? Did my husband? I never knew, I had no eyes to see the monsters battering against their confining bars, the torment of the wild things gnawing at themselves in their murderous agony.

I thought during the week of crisis Charlotte helped me to talk through, that I had been able to express a great deal of my built-up anger and frustration on the tapes we recorded. Now I can see that what I imagined was part of the cataclysmic bursting of the dam released only a minute fragment of the fury and hate that has been beating itself unceasingly against the confines where my mind has hidden it all my life, growing in strength, increasing in violence so that I was driven again and again to the point of suicide to get away from it.

When you are containing such a destructive force within yourself, when your aggressive instincts have been repressed to the extent that mine have been, when you are terrified to lose your temper, to give way to any form of anger because the power you will let loose seems as though it will destroy your whole world and yourself with it, there is a constant and exhausting battle waging deep within you that underlies everything you do in the apparently normal process of living.

I never, so far as I can recall, gave way to the 'temper tantrums' of childhood. Violence of any sort has sickened and frightened me all my life. I rarely complained about anything I found difficult or unsatisfactory. Others expressed their annoyance, kicked cars that broke down, fumed over having to wait in queues, told each other in loud voices that whatever got in their way 'wasn't good enough', was unfair, displayed gross incompetence.

I must have known from a very early age that nothing was fair and nothing was right, but I knew too that I had no means of putting my complaint forward since if I did, I would find out that the blame for whatever was wrong lay unequivocally with me. So when cars broke down, I gritted my teeth and said nothing, assuming the responsibility and cringing with guilt. When delays occurred, I was the one to apologise because everyone else was having to suffer inconvenience. With a sick sinking inside, I knew that everything that ever went wrong was bound in some way to be my fault. I never complained for myself – I had learned to endure in silence - and if other people were angry I tried to direct their anger at me so that I could admit a fault, humbly apologise and somehow wipe their aggression out.

But the sick feeling, the nausea and the shaking when anything went wrong must have been because deep down, my own unexpressed fury and hate was adding more and more fuel to itself – more and more things were not fair, not right, and why the hell should I be condemned to take them all on myself? Inside, I suppose I was screaming at the whole bloody unfairness of life. It hurt me to have to shoulder all blame in order to avoid having to try and cope with other people's anger when I was unable to retaliate. It wounded me to the heart, pierced me to the soul, and the hate, the fury I contain somewhere inside the recesses of my mind is for countless hurts, unfairnesses, injustices, wrongs, humiliations, crawling apologies for things that were not my fault, which I have had to suffer in silence for forty-three years simply because I was never able to stand up for myself and release my own aggression.

*

Even though I think I have a strong will and am capable of taking command, of leadership and organisation, I am utterly unable to handle physical or mental violence. I will do anything to avoid it.

I had two years of steadily increasing depression and despair after the birth of my daughter that brought me to the same point of breakdown I was to come to know so well later. Manic energy thrashing about for a way out, a sensation of being trapped in circumstances that were unbearable, frustration and bewilderment that were even worse then because I had no experience of them to such a debilitating degree. Call it post-natal depression in order to give it a label – whatever it was, no-one recognised it, even my doctor, though I pleaded with him for help.

I had no drugs to take – no-one had any idea I might be needing them even though I was displaying all the now familiar symptoms of chronic stress. Then one day when things were particularly bad and my daughter, then two-and-a-half, irritated me beyond the limits of what I felt I could endure with some small naughtiness, I let fly and slapped her face. I'm haunted by that incident of desperation and failure to this day. I had actually hurt my own little girl quite unnecessarily because I couldn't handle the hurts within myself.

I was seized with a terrible fear that I might do her even more damage, that I might actually break her bones, throw her out of the window, murder her, though in fact I would probably have killed myself first. What was so frightening was that I had actually hit her at all, that I had lost control of my anger to the extent that it had found a physical outlet. I had never struck her before that one occasion, and I never hit her again.

I have never, so far as I can remember, ever hit anything or anyone – even pet dogs or cats. It takes the most immense and overwhelming pressure to bring me to the point where I feel even the urge to strike out. I have lost my temper only once in my life, and the violence of that awful few minutes shook me with trembling that seemed like a convulsive fit. I was terrified of the destructive force of my fury and hate and took care for years afterwards that never, however far I was driven, would I lose control again. Whatever had been originally planted in my mind as a prohibition became consciously intensified. I knew I was incapable of handling my anger. I forced myself to swallow it, not to retaliate, never, never to lose my cool, to stay patient, to keep calm, to keep quiet.

Even in dreams, I struggled against it. I often dreamed – particularly as time went on – that I was being attacked or threatened in some way and needed to strike out, hit back. In the dream I would lift my hand and it would freeze, I would be unable to move it. I could not strike, even in my unconscious mind.

So far as I am aware at the moment I have two distinct reactions to this inability to hit back. One perhaps explains the great fears that haunt me, the terrors I can't identify, the sensation that something is waiting to pounce, a shadow of incomprehensibly monstrous and awful proportions that lurks somewhere just outside my line of vision. When it comes it will crash through stones, bricks, barriers – nothing will be able to keep it out or keep it from annihilating me and I am afraid because I feel myself defenceless in the face of whatever may happen. I know I cannot fight back however much I am threatened.

Sometimes, walking along a street, I feel such terror of other people – women as well as men – that I can hardly force my legs to keep moving in order to pass them. My knees shake, my whole instinct is to turn and run away screaming. I go rigid, my muscles stiffen and will not work, the panic almost knocks me over. I feel my limbs are out of control and it is only by the most intense effort of concentration and will that I can take the necessary steps forward to keep me moving.

I often wondered during the period when I tried vainly to protect myself in my dreams whether, if I should actually be physically attacked – mugged, raped – I would be able to try and hit back in order to defend myself. Even though I am aware of some of the tricks that can – if one is lucky – repel an attacker I doubt whether I am physically able to strike back with intent to incapacitate or hurt, even in self-defence. Mercifully I have never been put to the test. I think an experience like that would shock and outrage me so much that the increased anger and hate in my mind might make it impossible for me ever to recover. It might quite literally send me into madness. And I fear all the time that it may happen.

The second reaction comes as a result of being unable to express my anger and it is very common to sufferers of depression, probably of other mental illnesses as well. It is the utter exhaustion, the mental tiredness of trying to struggle against the violence in your mind. Whether this is done consciously or unconsciously, the conflicts within yourself that by their very nature never stop or give you a single moment's respite from the constant battle you are waging deep down where no-one can see it, drain you so that you are too weary to be able to think, to cope, to make any effort at all.

Any form of repeated frustration – not necessarily to do with mental illness – has this same effect to some degree. Anger and hate have to be contained, you are not allowed to express them but they are there all the same, worrying at you like a dog gnawing at a bone, driving you into dead-ends, taking you over so that the ordinary civilities of life become of secondary importance. You are fighting within yourself for your own survival.

*

Last night I scribbled:

'Very late now. Thought I was doing so well. Have been clear of that yawning nothingness since the breaking of the dam, the traumas with Charlotte. Swept back over me just now. Misery – desolation – hopelessness. Why am I writing this? I'm so tired, so sick inside. My chest hurts, my throat is full of tears I can't weep. Why am I trying so hard? Where am I going? These pages – so difficult – I am shaking all the time, sick all the time from the anger as I describe it. I'll never let it out. I'll never be free of it. Why bother? Why try to make sense of it all? What is the point of everything? I am so very tired.

'A homeless cat turned up a few days ago at the flats where we live. Not a sweet kitten, a full-grown cat with long fur rather matted. He was very hungry. He had fleas. Mutely followed everyone who passed him, trying to gain comfort from contact with human beings. Asked for so little, just care, just reassurance that he was wanted in the world. A lovely cat, so friendly, so trusting. I wanted to take him in. Impossible.

'That evening all the theories in the book didn't work. I went into deep withdrawal. D and I spent two hours not talking. He was worried about the cat too, but we cannot have it. We've found a home for it though – everyone at the flats rallying round – but then the trouble started. 'It's got fleas!' 'We can't have it wandering round in the corridors!'

'Maybe his new owner won't keep him now. Oh God, how I hate human beings, how I loathe myself because I am helpless. I wasn't even able to assert myself to the extent of being permitted to rescue a lost cat. '*YOU ARE NOT ALLOWED TO DO IT*.' The same old story. I cannot, I must not, I am not allowed. Rules, regulations, prohibitions over which I have no control. The face of love that is a mask for my murderer. The smile that conceals the dagger poised to strike.

'Don't trust them, little cat, they will turn and kick you out back into the dark and the cold because you aren't sleek and satisfactory and freed of your fleas. Oh, God, I wish I could save you. Your lostness is breaking my heart.'

3
DESCENT INTO THE DEPTHS

From 'Tanya's' discussions of her progress with 'Charlotte', recorded on tape.

Charlotte: Tanya, I know that writing this book…what you are doing…has been – still is – intensely traumatic.
Tanya: Yes, in fact I'm not at all sure whether I'm helping myself to uncover the traumas of the past and hopefully face them, or whether I'm driving myself further into stark raving insanity, where I shall be lost for evermore. I have been having feelings I've never experienced before, which may or may not be some new sort of depression – there are different types of depressions, as you know, having suffered yourself.
Charlotte: A sort of black pit?
Tanya: The colour goes out of the world.
Charlotte: You slow down; nothing's ever going to be right.
Tanya: An absolute despair. I know it so well, almost a way of life – and, although you know it will pass, it seems as though it never will. You get to understanding the way it works…but, apart from that, I've also been experiencing – possibly through consciously trying to think myself into my problems – other sensations that I thought at first were different, new depressions… but I'm not sure now whether they are actually depressions at all. I can't really say what they are.
Charlotte: Can you describe them?
Tanya: Not very clearly. They've been coming so slowly that I didn't notice them to start with, but the other day I had the

worst so far. I tried to describe it immediately afterwards, write down what it felt like: this is what I wrote:

I thought I'd touched bottom, the depths – but now the bottom gets deeper, the depths of lostness and pain become unfathomable. I can't speak, I can't scream or cry or hold onto anything or anyone. My whole body is a mute vessel into which the pain pours, fills to the brim, cannot express itself. I have no words, no tears. I ache – throb – exist as a single unit of pain.

This is past despair, past desperation, depression, past the sickness of the soul that I thought I could not bear. I have known nothing like it. It is not living, it is not death. There are no words for me to describe it. I cannot compare it to anything. It is so utterly, utterly negative, such a state of sick nothingness that no images I can conjure up are powerful enough. Agony is positive – it provokes a reaction. This provokes nothing. It is the unendurable, which I must endure until I can find the strength to struggle free, to come back to words, consciousness of reality.

…That's so inadequate, though, Charlotte. I was floundering. I simply couldn't use words which would describe the feeling – I couldn't find any. It seemed a sort of sensation – experience – whatever it was – that was completely unfamiliar. As though I'd been somewhere, some place…that I had never, ever, known in my life.

It certainly wasn't death. I was not dying, I wasn't dead, but it was some…I can't even find the right words now.

I could not… utter... No sound. The comparisons, the images I tried to think of were simply… oh, removed, utterly removed. I thought of…oh, the Arctic – wolves howling – and then I said to myself, no, that's much too *positive*. The images of trapped animals howling were far too positive. None actually explained it, got anywhere near it.

I thought of just one shriek of pain, one scream of pain – but there *was* no shriek, no scream. I can't find one single right word for '*it*', whatever or wherever it was or might have been. Just pain, nothingness, lostness, awfulness … But none of them is right.

Charlotte: There were no physical familiarities?

Tanya: No. It was very frightening, because it seemed a place that I'd never ever conceived or known of or imagined. I couldn't begin to describe it at all, and it was worse for not being able to be expressed in any way of which my five senses are capable. It can't be expressed in any other form than by living it, that's all I can say really. But *what* I was living, I don't know.

Charlotte: How did you feel when you came out of it? Have you any idea how long it lasted?

Tanya: I don't think it was very long, because I made an effort – I tried to…well, come back, I suppose. In the beginning, everything faded and I was able to take in very little of what was going on around me - (I was sitting at the table in the kitchen with D., actually, and we were having supper). In depression, of course, one normally isn't very interested, but this wasn't so much not being interested, it was as though everything faded into the distance.

I might have been spoken to; if I was I don't think I answered. I couldn't speak. And afterwards, well, I wanted to speak, but I was afraid I couldn't get back to the words, use my voice. I couldn't speak for…oh, half an hour.

I was crying, even though I wasn't consciously crying…a few very slight tears were just running down my face. I wanted to cry, and I couldn't, because I couldn't express myself in any way. I could move – I was able to walk, but only if I was led. I knew I had got to come back…

I felt as though I couldn't really hold onto anything, even though D. sat with me. I shook, quite violently…gasped, took big gulps as though I'd been drowning and come up for air. Eventually, it all wore off.

But all these were part of my reaction, they weren't the 'thing' itself. I had got perhaps halfway back by the time I'd reached what I've just described…

What I wanted more than anything was to be able to cry. I knew I would be making contact with normality when I could do that, and I had to cry something out. And I did say to D. – it's not easy to remember what happened now – but I know I said: 'I've been very far away. I've been very deep.' And then I said: 'It is much more painful than I thought, there is a lot of pain somewhere down there.' And then I said: 'Terrible, terrible pain', and after I had managed to say just these few words, get them out, I was able to cry.

Charlotte: In fact you've been into an area not of physical pain but of mental pain that's perhaps far more unendurable. Physical pain can actually be endured.

Tanya: I wonder sometimes about mental and physical pain. I mean, this 'thing' – if there's somebody – God forbid, but if there are people living in that sort of pain, they'd be better dead, I reckon. I can't even describe the pain -. Depression is a pain – it's a pain in the neck – but it wasn't just depression – I mean depression's my old friend really -.

Charlotte: Compared.

Tanya: Yes. Oh, yes, this was something absolutely horrifying. What did go through my mind afterwards – the only thing at all that came anywhere near to provoking a similar reaction in me – and even this might be too imaginative, because it's something personal to me, to my own reactions to things —I'm thinking of Salvador Dali – I've always regarded the Surrealists with a certain dreadful fear because their landscapes are so – threatening, so inexplicable, menacing, strange. The 'thing' wasn't like that, but perhaps it had a certain similarity. Does that explain at all to you?

Charlotte: Yes, it explains a lot. The Salvador Dali image doesn't work with me though, because most of the things I've seen are so harshly coloured they don't seem to have any affinity with what you've been describing.

Tanya: No, not the colours, that's not what I mean, the ability to evoke a sense of – of cruelty and horror -.

Charlotte: But from what you've said, I imagine their images are still too positive.

Tanya: Certainly the colours. I couldn't attempt to describe any colours. If I go there again, I might try, but I'm certainly not going to wish it on myself, though the experience - the sensation – has happened more than once, but at first it was sort of – insidious – slight. What I was describing was the worst time. But if that's where I've got to go to find it all out, I shall go I suppose.

There are other images I've had when I've been thinking myself into the pain and the depression – into the lostness and the rejections and the desolations. It might be my mind again though, putting the sensations into form, but I've had images of a place which is somewhere else I don't recognise – much less indescribable – vaguely of rocks, like bones -. I'd better not do this, I don't think, because I really can't be sure you know, it's difficult afterwards. But I have had the images of somewhere – I can't say desolate or alien, those are not strong enough words – a place again that I don't know – perhaps the sea, water, rocks, skeletons, bones – I can't really put it into words, not now, it isn't recent enough. I've had the feelings or whatever but I didn't write them down. Now I try to describe where I think I go, afterwards. But it isn't easy because, for one thing, I'm afraid of it coming back as I write

– and if it doesn't come back as I'm recalling it, I think I haven't got it like it was because I can't remember it properly.

Charlotte: That's a 'double bind' if you like.

Tanya: Well, I did the best I could. I couldn't possibly have described it when I was in it, but I did it straight away after, and whether what I've been able to say is of any help to anyone – whether it's going to be of any help to me – I don't know.

*

Tanya continues her Book:

Charlotte and I discussed the 'descent into the depths' in conversations that were not, unfortunately for me, recorded. We couldn't record everything. What was the significance of it all? What could it mean? Neither of us is trained in psychology or psychiatry, so our conclusions are only tentative, and must be regarded as the tentative groping of lay minds.

Apart from drugs and a certain amount of talking, though never any concentrated 'psychoanalysis' as such, other treatments I have had in the past to help me to try to function normally are ECT – electro-convulsive-therapy – and relaxation therapy. But the drugs, the ECT, the relaxation, even the talking, can never provide any basic 'cure' for what is wrong with me. They merely ease the symptoms – the shaking, the despair, the agitation, the misery.

The immediate reaction of the few people who know what I am writing – whether they have read the manuscript or not – is to ask whether I have been treated by hypnosis. I haven't. I was never offered hypnosis, and I felt in the past that I couldn't see how it would help me, since even Charlotte's black-humoured suggestion that I should be 'put under' for an hour and told repeatedly: "You *are* a good girl" would probably achieve nothing. A hypnotist cannot put anything into another's mind that their innate standards of morality, integrity, or whatever will not allow them to accept. I don't think for instance, that it is possible for anybody to persuade a person to commit murder by means of hypnosis. And in my case, somehow I knew that however much I might be told that everything was all right, that I had no need to worry, I would remain unconvinced.

One method of treatment that I did make enquiries about when I was in hospital was 'abreaction'. This is where by means of hypnosis (and, I think, drugs as well) the patient is taken back to re-live his basic traumas, the incident or incidents of the past that are so desperately painful that they are buried deep in the unconscious and cannot be faced. Once the original traumas can be brought to light, the idea seems to be that in 're-living' them, it is possible for the patient to be assisted to cope with them *at the time they happened*, so that the original pattern of behaviour which followed can be altered and it will no longer be necessary to hide from the pain and put up defences. It's like having the chance to live the difficult bits of your life over again, I suppose, and being given help to proceed in the right direction rather than the one which you originally ran screaming along in an effort to get away from the trauma, and which necessitated all the pain and depression and worry of later years.

When I asked whether I could have 'abreaction' I was told that I could if I liked, but the authorities felt it wouldn't really help me at all, and would only cause me a great deal of distress. Since I was able to see the logic – since there seemed to be no trauma or incident that had ever happened to me which could be 're-lived', since so far as I knew my childhood had been relatively happy and I had never been deprived or gone through any form of upheaval – I agreed that probably it was unnecessary.

But even then, the psychiatrists whom I have so loudly denounced were far wiser than I knew. In the first part of this book, I was still fighting against the idea that being aware of the frustrations and miseries in my past life would in any way be able to help me. At the same time, though, I was performing my own 'therapy' and taking myself back, doing my own form of 'psychoanalysis' as I tried to put myself, my thoughts, my feelings, in order.

Apart from being very painful, any form of analysis is also a lengthy process. I believe it has been said that no psycho-analytical picture of any substance can be considered complete until the treatment has been under way for years – it is supposed to take five years for a basic Freudian analysis. I can only conclude that in my case, I had long since stopped having any faith in psychiatrists and had been unconsciously working on my own mind myself.

In the books I have written over the years, I can see a pattern. Very slowly, without realising it, I was groping my way into a deeper understanding of myself, letting the externals – the descriptions of scenery, flowers, physical features and so on – drift away. I was becoming more and more concerned with the workings of the minds of my characters (which were, of course, expressions of me).

I must repeat that all of this, even when I started to write these opening pages, even when I stumbled to a standstill because I was too frightened to go further alone, finding it was drawing me into realms of pain I didn't understand and experiences that I couldn't interpret, which I thought might mean I had lost control of my mind and had actually gone insane without realising it – all of this happened without my conscious volition. The 'thing' I described to Charlotte had been occurring without my being able to will it to happen or realising it would happen at all and on top of my already extreme depression, these incredibly severe 'descents into the depths' were horrifying and appalling.

Before I talked to Charlotte, I didn't know whether I was going into a depth from which I might be able to crawl back to a more positive normality, or whether I was experiencing the first signs that my brain was actually disintegrating, that my logic and my reasoning powers were leaving me for ever, and that I was about to relinquish all forms of mental control over myself and be plunged into 'it' entirely, unable to think, speak, communicate with reality in any way.

*

Charlotte and I came to the conclusion that, impossible though it seems, I had already proceeded to regress to the period before I was old enough to have even the basic vocabulary of a small baby. I must have gone back to the earliest weeks – maybe even the earliest moments - of my life, possibly even into a recollection of when I was still in the womb, before I was born.

We think that what I experienced – what I call the 'thing' – must have been the original hurt, rejection, damage, or whatever it was, that scarred the little entity that was to develop into Tanya Bruce so that she was thereafter to remain crippled by it during all her years of living. What it might have been, I have no idea, and I don't think that anyone else could possibly know either. I had no words at my command to describe it, I only knew what it had felt like, which there is no way of communicating. I lived it – the most primitive, basic, fundamental 'it' being a consciousness simply of unendurable suffering, nothing else.

Afterwards I wrote:

'Most marvellous sense of relief, lightness of spirit, so relaxed after telling Charlotte about the 'descent'. This can only be a good sign. The colours are back in the world – I can touch things – see them. I am smiling as I write this – not the forced smile I've stretched my face into for so long. I feel free as air, I could dance for joy. I haven't known joy – even this tentative, hesitant joy that will probably disappear by tomorrow – for so long. I'd forgotten what joy felt like. Am I being reborn, given a second chance? Is this the beginning of the end – the end of the beginning?

'I'm sitting very still, savouring a stirring of hope. I'm not going to rush it in case I lose it. Tomorrow – tomorrow – I may be able to take another step along the way. Suddenly it seems the world is in focus a little. Maybe I belong here after all.

'Goodnight dear Charlotte, God bless you.'

4
A BLUEPRINT FOR LIVING

Instinctively now, as I have done for years as a writer, I trust my subconscious mind, and if I leave it alone to do its work, it never fails me. It 'writes' my books, weaving and dovetailing threads together in an incredible manner. It forgets no detail, however small. My subconscious is highly trained, a formidable weapon.

I wish I had no conscious mind, it interferes with the working of the machine, gets carried away, side-tracked, pressured, upset, hurt, depressed. I would like for many reasons to exist as nothing but a subconscious, what I jokingly described to Charlotte as 'just a brain on legs' – though even the legs might well be dispensable. My consciousness is a burden to me, so is my body, and I have reached a stage now where – most of the time – I can do little but get up, write until I am exhausted, try to rest, continue writing. Without something – a book, a play, a story – to work on, I have no purpose in life, it is empty and pointless, a dull chore that has to be got through somehow, though I see no reason in it.

I imagine this is why I became a writer, why I tried even as a young child to create my own worlds in my head which I could organise, control, shape into patterns that were somehow satisfying. Many writers are motivated in the same way, escape into fantasy worlds where the creator is God and is able to formulate order out of seeming chaos gives you an 'out' from the pain and incomprehensibility of reality.

I regard the real world – in words I have used previously – as my 'raw material', something to provide me with experience and knowledge with which to work. The one thing I have never agreed to relinquish in the whole of my life, at any time, has been my writing. Even if other people couldn't see its importance to me, I knew that I needed it just as much – if not more – than food and drink. I am addicted to words, to thoughts, to ideas. I devour them voraciously, I can never have enough.

I said to Charlotte that if I had been one of Pavlov's dogs, it would have been a typewriter rather than food at the other side of my cage. I get up, make meals, make conversation, do what I have to do in a practical way as though I am jumping a series of obstacles, all for the reward of the moment when I can sit with a fresh piece of paper in the machine, my hands poised, my brain fresh. That, to me, is the greatest happiness I have ever known. All else perishes – the balm of flogging one's guts out trying to create, never fails.

This book has turned into more than a record of the feelings of a mentally sick writer, for it has become obvious, judging by what happened – and what is still happening as I continue to chronicle the saga as best I can – that my subconscious has been working all the time for me on the problem I'd set myself, which I had no expectation could ever be dealt with in any satisfactory manner.

I started the early pages in the vague hope that I could help myself, sort myself out. My brain —though I didn't know it had done so – took up the challenge. It set me to work, guided me back through the past, through all the pain of childhood, it even led me 'into the depths' to uncover my fundamental, basic suffering, recreated for me the moment – hour – day – when that suffering occurred. Though I was overwhelmed – though it took some time to grasp what was happening – I could see if I tried to stand back a little that my brain had been working along the lines of normal analytical processes.

But after the mind has been taken back to face its deeply hidden traumas, I asked myself, what happens then? So maybe I've faced them – well, what now? Can there be more? What's going to happen next – or will nothing happen at all? I was very dazed, I simply waited, with no idea at all of what to expect – though I don't actually think I was expecting anything.

*

When it came, it was in about three definite flashes of self-realisation that my subconscious passed quietly into my conscious mind. They happened within a few days – perhaps two days – of discussion I had with Charlotte about the 'descent', and they came within hours of each other. I wrote them down on pieces of scrap paper, just as they were. I realised what each one meant, but I couldn't actually see the links, the patterns of what was being presented to me.

Not until the 'flashes' seemed to have stopped, and I was getting no more revelations to add to what I already had, was I able to evaluate what my brain had been doing. In essence, it had presented me with what I had been looking for when I started to write this manuscript. It had 'sorted me out' and it had found me a way to go, when there had previously been no way at all. What I was holding on my pieces of scrap paper was a blueprint, an outline uniquely programmed for Tanya Bruce on 'How to Live'.

Nothing has been solved, I have not been 'cured'. I think now that my problems are even worse than I had ever imagined, the task of having to apply my blueprint to the future is so monumentally difficult that it appears impossible. But at least I can see the road ahead, though whether I will be able to summon up the strength or the courage to make any headway along this road, I doubt very much at the moment. And I'm certain that even my blueprint isn't the complete answer. But the effort that it has taken to get this far has drained me. Perhaps when the shock waves of all the traumas have subsided, when the dust has settled, I may be able to do something positive, however small a step I take. At least I know now that the road is there.

*

When the first 'flash' came, I wrote down:

'The whole focus has shifted in me, not in the outside world, that's still the same. It's *ME*. I've seen myself for the first time as actually non-existent. The feeling that nothing was real, it wasn't the world that was insubstantial, it was *MYSELF*. The picture's turned upside down – I see not faults or blame – but the fact that I quite simply have no reality *TO MYSELF*. And the truth was there all the time.

'I can only live through others' need', I wrote. But it's taken on a new and terrible meaning now. I quite literally *DO NOT EXIST* to myself without that need. I am utterly dependent on what I fear, what I resent, what I have spent my whole life fighting – the limitations, the judgements, the requirements, the demands of people I do not understand and feel I despise and hate.

'To myself, I am nothing', I wrote. Now I see the truth, the real truth of what I meant, that's why I am so frightened.

'I'm faced with absolute nothingness inside myself, I'm aware of it, my lack of personal desires, wants, purposes, concern for what others regard as the expression of themselves. I have no self to express – or if I have, I've got to find it. The terrifying thing is not that I want to be free of being myself but that I turned round, I actually turned round

45

as Peggy Poole's poem expressed it, and looked at my pursuer, and when I faced myself, there was nothing there to face. It's like looking in a mirror at your reflection, and nothing looks back at you. It's empty.'

*

Stunned and shocked, I made a few more sketchy notes several hours later, using phrases from the manuscript, phrases I had written without realising what I had been saying, but which now seemed to ring with awful clarity like a knell of doom.

'I have no self – maybe you've realised at last no-one else will help you – you're your own best helper – but when I look for help in myself, there's nothing of me there to turn to - " - plastered into stars" – everyone taken a chunk – I exist in fragments – the characters in my books – the limitations of others -.'

'What's the problem? To bring the pieces together, to make a whole person, one who'll have to learn to cope alone? Can one do this – ?'

*

A few hours later:

'This must be what I have to do, collect the scattered pieces, the things that make up a person – desires, opinions, preferences, needs. I'll have to try and reach a point – I suppose – where something does actually matter to me – whether I like tea weak or strong, whether I prefer blue curtains to green, the myriad points which make a personality take on form and substance. I have never had preferences, what other people wanted came first. Can one persuade oneself that blue or green curtains, strong or weak tea, really matter? How do I do that? All seems to be important so far as I can see is that there is actually tea to drink – whether strong or weak – that there are actually curtains of whatever sort to draw across and keep out the dark and the cold. So many other people have opinions about these things. Why add another argument to what seems to me a pointless exercise? Let them have what they would like, it will make them happy. It makes no difference to me.

'The last time I was in a mental hospital – quite recently, but only for a week – one of the doctors or somebody said to me: "Oh, Tanya, when will you stop giving and take something for yourself?"

'It didn't seem much at the time. I think I've been as selfish as anyone else – I *do* take from others – I take a lot. But I think I see now what he was getting at. It's not so much a question of being selfish, but of being an actual self that's recognisable as such.'

*

Another brief 'flash':

'I resent my dependency, but when the people I love/hate go away – when D. isn't here – the limits lift and I am bewildered, I panic, I don't know what to do – I rush into a 'mania' – spend – I cannot cope except by returning to the limits 'they' – my mother, my husband, D. – impose on me, based on their own realities, which I so resent the rest of the time. An inability to cope with freedom of choice if the restrictions are lifted and I am actually free to choose for myself.

I am swamped by too much freedom, I run back to the limits laid down by 'them' – my love/hate objects. Yet when they are there, I'm always fighting to be free of them and unable to see how I need what I am fighting against. Sometimes I actively despise 'them' – I feel I am superior – I have vision they don't possess – they embarrass me, make me ashamed of them –

'Through their despised attention to the details that so irk me – strong or weak tea – blue or green curtains – laying the table, personal preference, I am able to eat properly, be gentle to myself, warmth, a little comfort - Without them I am just a brain -.'

*

The last 'flash':

'To discover yourself, maybe you have to give up everything – even the expectation of love from anybody, the actual *wanting* of that love, you have to lose all feelings, all desires, wants, needs, so that you ask for nothing at all from anybody. You can't do this easily – the letting go is overwhelmingly reluctant – the sense of losing the little you have, even the need to have it, makes you feel you will lose yourself. The terror, the fear is so real that you fight to retain at least *something*, some fragment, some atom of what is familiar. You cling even to your angers, your bewilderments, your very pain, you can't take that step into a completely dark unknown.

'It's made unconsciously. When it is done, then without your own volition, having made it, something else comes out of the void. A sense of power that grows, takes you by surprise. You don't expect it. You wonder at it. What is it? Can this be mine, this feeling?

'The expression that came to me was: "I am the master of my fate, I am the captain of my soul". I don't know yet – I have to find out, make tests, discover more. But perhaps for the first, the very first time I have done something for myself, completely unaided, I have done something on my own.

Look at me, look at me, I am at this moment in control, I am strong, I'm not driven by anything, no dictates – no desire to conform – no limitations set down by anyone else. I did it myself! And wherever I am, I got here under my own steam. 'I *am* the captain. *I* will choose – *I* will decide – I can! I can do it! The power is so wonderful, so thrilling, so exciting. I don't want to lose it – I hope it won't go away. I snap my fingers at everybody. I am *me* – I don't need you. I am *me*. I can stand alone, I can do it all myself. Laughing, uncaring, not afraid of you any more. Living. I'm me and I'm alive – I exist. Get lost, world, I can manage without you. I'm strong enough not to care any more.'

*

Exit to triumphal swelling of chorus by heavenly choir. End of story. It doesn't work like that. I didn't think it would. I've lived with the enemy for too long. Last night I wrote:

'Five to five in the morning. The dead hour before dawn once again. I typed up these last few pages yesterday. Afterwards I found myself thinking of my mother, as I saw her one day when I was a little girl, crying as she forced herself to drown our pet cat's new-born kittens, which we couldn't possibly keep nor find homes for, in a bucket of water. Kneeling with the little blind helpless things pushed mercifully deep, though the tears were pouring down her face and she was choking out: "Oh God, forgive me."

'I see not myself in the empty mirror but her guilt and her pain, the small ghosts that have haunted her own dark hours. She was just a child, just a child, and it tore her apart. So many things tore her apart.

'And my husband crying suddenly when Bing Crosby's voice on the radio started to croon about "the sweet white-haired lady I love". He had just lost his mother. He wanted her back. Overwhelming, terrible grief. That's there too, along with the drowning kittens and my mother's pain.

'I can't face it. I am nothing – I know that's the truth, nothing but other people's need, their fear, their anguish. How can I resolve it? It's too much, too much. I haven't slept. I thought of my mother and my husband and all night I wrestled with misery. The world is so full of suffering, and I can do nothing but grieve for the griefs of others. For myself, I don't care. I have no strength left to care. I am very tired, very exhausted, very depressed. It wasn't my own hurting but my helplessness to ease their pain that broke my heart.

'I don't want to go on. I don't want to try any more. The night is so long, so lonely. No sign of the dawn. Maybe when the day comes I'll be able to sleep. But there's no rest, no peace, only a gathering of strength to try and carry the load a bit further. One more night – one more day - . I must keep going. I've got to hang on. There must be some reason for it all.'

5
THE LINES ARE OPEN

During the six weeks or so that I have been involved in writing this book, much has happened that I couldn't begin to try and record, as well as what I have put down. The amount of thinking, of sorting facts, of trying to make sense of what I was doing, has been phenomenal. I have lived with my problems, unable to emerge from them, for almost the whole time, except to eat and sleep. In the beginning I did my thinking alone, supported by D.'s encouragement. In reading of my difficulties, he began to speak of his own, and for the first time we were able to communicate with our real selves, though rather slowly and painfully to begin with. We began to come closer, to understand each other better.

When Charlotte and I continued the voyage of discovery through our discussions, the pace stepped up. New ideas, new revelations, sparked off by her comments, surged into my mind. I have described the traumas that took place within a few days of her participation after we had talked for hours on the tapes. Every evening afterwards, I phoned her and told her what I had written, what I had been thinking, that day. And we continued to talk. All the time, I was concentrating – unable to help myself – getting swamped with self-realisation, awareness.

By the time I had reached my description of the 'flashes' or 'revelations' that seemed to make up the blueprint I have detailed, I felt I'd come to a full stop. I was physically exhausted and for two days afterwards, the unpleasant effects of extreme effort manifested themselves in chronic constipation followed (when I'd recognised the pains and taken an appropriate 'dose') by uncontrollable and chronic diarrhoea, coupled with the usual nervy trembling, weakness, and other nasty symptoms that are so much less 'romantic' or 'dramatic' than mental suffering which takes place outside the world of inexplicable rashes deforming one's face, itching so that people think you've got the plague, and frantic visits to the loo. All of these, though, will be familiar to sufferers from chronic stress, whether mental or not.

But by then, the lines of communication were well and truly open – not only open, but humming. D. and I were talking deeply, and the understanding I had not expected from anyone – least of all, I think, from him – overwhelmed me. He too had moved a long way since I started the first pages of Chapter One. And Charlotte and I carried on, after a few days rest, where we had left off.

What follows is taken from a further marathon of talking which we again recorded. We too had drawn closer in the weeks when she and D. had been helping me to make my journey into self-awareness, closer than we have ever been in the fifteen years we have known each other. By now I was beginning to feel the strain, beginning to weaken, but as I became more unable to tackle sorting things out myself, they both – again, to my somewhat bewildered amazement – drew near to lend me strength and wisdom.

In my world at the moment, I have them – metaphorically speaking – one on each side of me, not forcing me in any way, but giving me confidence that I do not possess in myself, and holding out love that, for perhaps the first time in my life, I feel tentatively that I may be able to accept since they are demanding nothing back except what I want to give. It is their faith in me, their belief in me, that is guiding my hands now on the typewriter keys. Alone, I think I would have given up the struggle. They are bringing me through.

Charlotte: I think it's time we did a bit of stock-taking now. I wondered how you feel now we've arrived where we have, since you've been able to clear the picture – or paint the picture. Where do we go from here? What are the particular problems that need to be resolved or over-come, as you see them? My own feeling is that you'll probably have to learn to live with them, but in a different way to the way you've done up to now. How do you see things yourself?

Tanya: Well, it's been – what? – two weeks since the 'revelations' and the 'blueprint' came to me, and my first reaction, my main reaction was one of extreme horror and absolute despair. I simply could not see any way in which my problems could be put right. As you say, in all probability, it's going to be a case of learning to live with them, but possibly treating them differently and handling them differently. I don't think they're ever going to go away at all. But I feel that what I do have now, which I didn't have before, is – I don't know if I dare actually say it at this point, but I do feel that in a way I have learned to know myself. To a certain extent. I don't feel I could get much further into myself.

One thing that's changed - In the very beginning of this manuscript I wrote in terrible despair that no-one was ever going to know me – no-one would ever understand me – well, now that I feel I understand myself, that has eased quite a lot. It doesn't worry me so much – I don't mind it so desperately - I suppose if you feel you know yourself as honestly as you can, there isn't the need to impose that self on others, or make them notice you. I don't feel so much that I want other people to have to understand me, because in whatever state I am, whether I'm fragmented or in bits and pieces, I'm still there whether they notice me or not, and that I think is the most tremendous step forward that I've made.

Charlotte: Yes, if you know yourself, it isn't so devastating when you realise that other people are never going to know you completely. Nobody ever knows anybody else completely. We know ourselves possibly, we can have some clear assessment of ourselves, though we can be too critical with ourselves. It's like when someone has a – well, experience – whether it's a vision or what, like Joan of Arc, she's the only obvious example I can give. But if you had something like that – and lots of people do have that sort of thing – I'm not talking of imbalance of mind, I'm talking of genuine vision. If you know you've had it, the true person who's had something like that does not mind at all whether other people don't believe him or her, because they know it's the truth, that it happened, and that's what matters.

Tanya: Well, when we started the discussions – when I'd got into such dreadful difficulty and the pain of trying to I suppose go back and psychoanalyse myself in whatever instinctive or unknowing way I was doing this – when it got too much, I did feel all along that what was happening was very similar to what you've just said. I felt that the thing we've called the 'descent' – at the time, it seemed very inexplicable and frightening, but I did have a feeling about it that I couldn't have explained. I felt, well, this is something which is the truth – as you say – I can't describe it as 'reality', but it was something positive and true in a way, however painful. I suppose it might be difficult for some people even to believe it happened, or that it wasn't simply an aberration – imagination – delusion – whatever - But *I* know where I went, and I know that it was something which gave me – I don't know what, but I feel I faced up in some way to myself, and I choose to think that it was that early pain, and that I went back consciously and accepted it and chose to accept it, and in so doing, I proved something to myself.

Charlotte: Just now when I was asking you about how you saw your difficulties, you made a very positive statement that's in direct contrast to how you said you saw things earlier on in our discussions. You said: 'Whether other people know me or not, I am still there.'

Tanya: Yes.

Charlotte: We started these discussions with you not being there at all.

Tanya: I think when we started the discussions, I didn't know whether I was there or whether I wasn't -

Charlotte: But now you *do* know you're there.

Tanya: When I went through the 'revelations' or 'insights' or whatever we call them, I came to see – as I wrote in the manuscript – that I did not in my own mind exist, and I existed in fragments. And yet, strangely -

Charlotte: You're beginning to put those pieces together now.

Tanya: Maybe I am, but I don't know how, because I'm not doing it in any conscious way. I suppose, though, I feel that even if I'm only existing in fragments – or in an empty mirror – at least I *am* existing.

*

Tanya: I don't know how the depressions, the angers, the 'manias' are going to be affected by what discoveries I've made so far, or whether they'll respond to a different outlook. So far as my personality goes – my own personality – I think I have some very basic and severe personality disorders. Well, that's obvious from the manuscript, and it's even clearer to me now, and I don't know whether they'll ever clear up or not.

Charlotte: What are you thinking of particularly?

Tanya: Well, for one thing, as I mentioned in the manuscript, I got to the point where I found a physical existence practically unbearable. I wanted to turn myself into just a brain, and whether that shame and loathing of myself, my physical person, is ever going to go away, I don't know. Maybe one can live with that up to a point, but it's certainly there. The dislike of being a body, a living body, has been with me – oh, from right back to the very early days – the days of not being allowed to look into the mirror and so on –

EDITOR: Tanya had earlier described an extremely repressive upbringing regarding her physical growth and a pervading sense of shame and sin

– and I don't really think it's possible to change someone's thinking so drastically – to the point, I mean, where I'll suddenly begin to enjoy staring at myself in a mirror and going completely the opposite way. One can only change oneself so much.

Charlotte: I don't think that if you were actually given the choice, you would want to turn into the sort of person who was very much preoccupied with her body, that is not the sort of person you are. Hopefully, you will learn to accept your body as part of the chassis – the holder, the surround of the engine of a car – or bodywork surrounding it, you know what I mean - . It's there, but you're never going to be the type of person who's going to spend a lot of time and thought working out how to adorn it, or decorate it or anything else. You've got a serviceable body – for which I suspect you're deep down thankful – you're not crippled or anything - .

Tanya: Oh, don't, when I think about handicapped and crippled people, I get another surge of guilt because I'm not crippled and yet I'm still moaning. My physical health must be – thank God – very tough, or else I expect I'd have ulcers or something from the mental stress and worry.

Charlotte: I don't think you have to overload importance on the body. Okay, it's a way of getting around and being part of this world where your brain lives. Your brain lives in your body; it's a house. Some people spend a lot of time in their houses – some don't.

Tanya: Yes, I see that, but at the moment, you know, I'm still very reluctant to actually decide – for good and all, I mean – whether to accept the world – and my body – and whatever else. I suppose in a way, by admitting that I exist, I've made some sort of decision already without knowing it - .

Charlotte: I shouldn't worry what you decide to accept. Your body's gone along for – what? – forty years without being accepted, and I'm sure it'll carry you on. You do tend it – you do wash – see to your hair – that's fine, that's all right.

Tanya: Maybe that's not going to be such a big difficulty.

Charlotte: No, I don't think it is. As long as you don't feel you have to make an over-emphasis on it, because that would be a nonsense and not in tune with the 'you' that I know – or the writer, the 'you' that I want to know.

*

Tanya: Perhaps my main difficulty is to do with the fact that, so far as I am aware, and always have been, I've never really been able to form so-called 'normal' relationships with other people. I don't know what's caused this – it could be the basic pain, whatever it was, that happened very early on – I think it's quite common to a lot of mentally ill people. I find it very difficult to have any relationships with people at all – and they don't follow what I believe are the normal patterns. For one thing, with my mother and then various 'authority figures' following on up to the present, I have always had to – where I loved – hate as well. Maybe that is going to put itself right, I don't know. Maybe it will ease without my having to do anything about it.

It's amazing really that in the space of two weeks – whatever it is – since we actually started to talk – and I would never have believed this possible, because for forty-three years I've been struggling against the sickness, the problem without any real alleviation of the distress - but things are going on inside me and in my head which I'm finding I don't know about until they've happened, and I seem to be moving forward whether I want to or not. I mean, decisions are being made at a staggering rate, and how this sort of thing could have happened within two – three weeks, I would have never ever been able to contemplate. Maybe other people – you know, when a cure, or what seems to be a cure happens for other people when they've been as ill as I have for forty years – possibly a cure *can* happen in three weeks – I don't know – but it seems utterly, utterly fantastic and unbelievable, and I'm really reeling from the shock. But things are *still* going on and decisions are being made in my head which I'm not actually controlling. I'm not consciously saying, Well, I'm going to change my outlook on how I feel about my body, for instance – or other people-

Charlotte: No, but you've opened the gates of the field, or the road or the house or whatever – wide! And a whole heap of things are coming in. It's exciting – it's also frightening – and maybe there will come some dust in as well as the good things – perhaps that's not the right way of expressing it – but as well as all the unexpected new slants, outlooks, possibly. It appears to have happened in three weeks, but that's only because within that three weeks you've consciously embarked on this, but the thinking, the sorting out has actually been going on much longer.

Tanya: It's true, but it's difficult in some ways for me to see exactly what is happening, as I think – consciously as well as unconsciously – on so many different levels. I mean, with the rational, logical part of me, I'm able to stand back and grasp implications, perhaps, evaluate and weigh them up even as I'm writing – I do this all the time in my other books, of course. But when you're trying to talk about something that's actually happening to *you* – trying to put that into some sort of readable form that makes sense, rather than a torrent of mad out-pouring, a 'stream of consciousness' type of thing, I'm also realising for instance that the sane and sensible advice I am able to give with one part of my mind, it's something completely foreign and unable to register at all.

Going back to the manuscript, I said – and I meant it, because it's out of my own experience – that it isn't a good idea to smother anybody with sympathy and try to cope for them. And yet, I'm aware that I am, or have been in the past, terribly guilty of doing exactly this. I'm seeing patterns cropping up everywhere. My mother followed this pattern with me – I can see it so clearly now, she took all choice from me, instead of letting me face my own decisions and accept my own responsibilities. And I've always been the same.

I drive my daughter frantic, she says: "Mum, stop fashing, you're pestering me." Mercifully, she's able to say this straight out – she doesn't just smoulder and resent me. But when I think back, I start to worry about how much harm I might have done my husband, or my daughter when she was little, I mean, I start thinking: Did I make their lives such a misery for them? And all so very well meant, trying so hard to please and to help. And there's a constant sifting and weighing up and forming of ideas and putting pieces together all the time I'm writing, in the way that I'm trained to do as a writer, and also in the way I'd work on any theory or something that I happened to want to think about.

But while that's going on 'up top', as it were, the part of me where all these 'descents' and emotions and feelings are, which must be far lower down, I suppose, on a more basic level, well, they're unaware of the fact that I must have been doing a lot of spadework in my mind over the years before I actually reached this point. This part of me is still reeling from *my own* 'revelations', and staggered because, I imagine, the universal truths, or whatever the 'revelations' largely consist of, have actually registered on my feelings and my emotions for the first time in my life. I don't suppose anything at all I've discovered is terribly original, and it was probably staring everyone else in the face all the time, but it had never dawned on *me* in such a way that I could actually accept it as applied to Tanya Bruce and not the rest of the world.

I seem to be split into different parts that don't interact with each other. As though maybe my brain grew up, but my emotions didn't, they just stopped dead somewhere a long way back. And now that possibly my emotions are starting to grow a little bit – if that's what they are doing – it's all very amazing and frightening and seems to be something that's just happened to me – thump – thump – thump – over the last few weeks since we started to talk. And apart from having any clinical sort of theoretical reaction, my main *feeling* is like I said, just shock and utter amazement that whatever has happened could have happened so – well, seemingly to my *feelings* – fantastically quickly.

Charlotte: I think it's perfectly clear that even at the beginning of the book, when you felt you didn't know what you were doing – when you had no idea what was going to happen, or whether anything would happen – you were already thinking things out in a very positive way. Our discussions were like the -

Tanya: Catalyst?

Charlotte: Yes, but you'd come to a point where you had to concentrate wholly on this, to the exclusion of all else, which is what you've been doing for three weeks, apart from the odd meal and attention to the nitty-gritty of living, going to bed and so on. You have been totally concentrating on this to – again, I think, a very brave extent, because it *has* been a journey into the unknown, something that neither of us expected or anticipated – and you're the one who's been at risk, not me. You didn't know where you were going to end up.

Tanya: No, and even as things happened they didn't seem to be making any sense at all, it was only afterwards that I could try to add them up, and see that something positive *had* been happening, that I'd actually been making some kind of progress through what appeared to be chaos. Gaining what I said earlier on, maybe, that little bit more self-knowledge.

*

Charlotte: This question of relationships – it's obviously a very serious problem. I think it's a result – a very natural and obvious result – of all that's happened in your life, and it's a very long-standing thing. I do feel though, that having sorted out so much, your realisations – your new discoveries – helping your whole perspective, that particular big problem may start now to become less -.

Tanya: Acute?

Charlotte: Less destructive, if you like. The poet Dannie Abse says somewhere that 'Everything profound abhors a mark'.

Tanya: What does that mean?

Charlotte: Well, it means basically, I think – and I feel he's right, that's why the quotation stayed in my head – there are two types of things. Sometimes a thing is much clearer, or sometimes it is diminished, by being labelled – sometimes it is very dangerous to do that.

Tanya: Yes, I see. The sort of way one could, for instance, add up a certain set of feelings or symptoms and 'label' them by saying: 'I have a cold', which would reduce the shakiness and the aching head and the runny nose and so on into something, as you say, much less, much diminished, even though true. But if somebody tried to add up – if I tried – to reduce my feelings about relationships into something with a label, it would be entirely different -. Maybe that's why – like I mentioned very early on in the manuscript – psychiatrists won't give mentally ill people labels to stick on themselves – why my doctor wouldn't give me a straight answer when I asked her if I was a manic-depressive – I mean, it's not as straightforward as a cold -.

Charlotte: The truth of what he said, the understanding one has is instinctive here, and not theoretical, I think.

Tanya: Something profound, maybe, shouldn't be tampered with – it should not be narrowed -.

Charlotte: It shouldn't be put in a box and labelled. You've got to be careful of it. And I think this particular area – relationships – is something that comes into that category. I don't want us to – so to speak – delineate it, mark it, diminish it, capture it. I suspect you will find that it will begin to become less of a worry. It's perfectly obvious to anybody, even without training or anything else, that as a small child you are always trying to win approval and seldom managed to, and after a certain length of time, it came into your head that you might as well stop trying. Again obviously, you resented the person whose approval you wanted to win and who wouldn't give it to you, so while loving them very much, you came to – as you say – hate them as well. Then you imposed that pattern, probably, on your other relationships because it had become the way you had learned to handle things. I don't know how much sense there is to you in that.

Tanya: Oh, it's absolutely true. The pattern has gone on all my life, and I feel – from my point of view – that people are completely unreliable -.

Charlotte: Do you ever hate your daughter?

Tanya: Do I ever – hate my daughter? I'm thinking -.

Charlotte: You've said that all your relationships are a mixture of love and hate. Do you hate your daughter?

Tanya: Well, when I was looking after her and bringing her up as a baby, a young child, I resented it because I felt that I was 'on duty', as it were, twenty-four hours of every day of every week -.

Charlotte: I think that's perfectly normal, especially with young Mums.

Tanya: I resented her in a way because she took over and denied me the chance to do – well, what I felt I wanted to do. But this pattern has been the same with everybody else -.

Charlotte: You're running away from my question and your answer. What you've been saying about your feelings towards your daughter when she was a child, is common to most Mums. They're tired, they've been unable to carry on with the work they might have been doing – most Mums, I think, have been very near to – if not actually battering their children at times, very near to it – from exhaustion, frustration – oh, ahh! I can't think of the right words, but you know what I mean. Shut in the house twenty-four hours a day, not sleeping properly because you have to see to the baby, the food you provide gets thrown on the floor – all the rest of it -. But that is not a long-term thing. And when – in your case – someone else took over the care of your daughter, when the pressures were off you – have you ever hated her?

Tanya: No, I don't think I have ever hated her, not at all. But what I did feel if I'm absolutely honest was that when I went back to her -. I couldn't keep away from her, because I wanted always to see her, I felt extremely guilty because I was not able to cope and bring her up myself, and I always looked forward to seeing her, I always wanted to see her – but when I got back, when I was with her, I would find it difficult to relate to her. After the joy of seeing her, I would find that I didn't know quite what to do. I could talk to her – but it's been the same really with everybody. I've always wanted to get to them, but when I get there, I find -. The fact that they love me, that my daughter loved me, that she was so obviously pleased to see me, that she would be waiting for me, it was lovely, and yet, I can't accept that from people. I find I want to run away from it – the burden of their affection is too much, and I can't cope with it.

Charlotte: You feel they're going to trap you in their ways, their mores, their pattern of behaviour, their habits. You feel that if you get too close, that's what will happen.

Tanya: With everybody, I want at first to get very close – I'll rush in, with anybody, friends, new acquaintances – I'll go to extreme lengths to make contact and to understand them and know them, but there always comes a point where I think to myself: Uh-huh, hang on. And I back out, I want to get away. Like I said, it's a burden, something I can't handle. For one thing, I find it very difficult to take anything from anybody – I find it very difficult even to take affection – or love. I want the love desperately, and yet at the same time, I get positively irritated and upset by any expressions of that love. I don't want them. But of course, you can't say that to people – you can't turn around and say: Well, I don't want you today, don't come near me today, I don't want to be near you and I don't want you to come near me. So what I suppose I do is just go along in as normal a way as possible, going through the motions -.

Charlotte: While at the same time building up a panic inside.

Tanya: No, not a panic. What I do is – if it isn't possible to withdraw physically, to go away somewhere, you know, alone, which of course isn't always possible – you can't run away from people so easily – what I do is simply to withdraw into my self. And then whatever they say or do or give me – expressions of affection like a kiss or a handshake, or whatever it is – I do what's expected of me in return, but there's a barrier inside myself. Really, I'm pretending, and a lot of my life I've done this because I've not wanted their love or affection. Yet in the beginning, I go madly in because I need it desperately, but once I've got it, I don't want it. This might be because – well, it might sound stupid, but what I'm doing, I suppose, is the equivalent of 'getting my own back' for what was done to me. That was what happened to me. I was – forced – coaxed – made – or maybe not forced at all – early on, maybe I just wanted to love people – and of course, they were people on whom I was dependent – I suppose it was only natural that I wanted to love them – I did love them. And they did this same thing to me. They made me love them – and then they took it away. Do you think that makes sense?

Charlotte: Yes, I think it makes perfect sense.

Tanya I don't do this consciously, of course. I don't wish it. I don't perhaps want to go away -. I can remember for instance when my daughter was small, I used to hug her and cuddle her because I loved her, and it was lovely when she responded. But – oh, God, when I think now what damage I might have done to her – I only hope it wasn't like the sort of thing that's affected me so deeply, but I couldn't – looking back, I couldn't possibly have done any different, even if I had the chance – I can't do it -. After the first breakdown, I still loved her, but I felt differently about – not about giving her the hugs and cuddles myself – I could do that – but I found it practically impossible to accept what *she* gave – her expressions of affection. I never turned them away, but the barrier was up inside – I didn't *want* her to burden me with hugs – not deep down. I suppose *I* could still express love, but I didn't want anyone to do it back. I'm just glad that at least she had two good years before things got difficult for her – maybe she had a better basis to build her feelings about relationships on than I did, because with me, I feel it must have been very much earlier on – it's so difficult to know.

Charlotte: But because of whatever it was that happened to you as a child, you feel you don't trust people?

Tanya: No, I do not trust anybody. Nobody.

Charlotte: That is because of the original rejection of your own love, and why you cannot dare to go on – once you've rushed in and, so to speak, extended love and it starts to come back to you – then is the danger point in your mind. If you go on offering love it might be thrown back at you, and so you're the one who wants to get out quick. You don't trust what's going to happen between yourself and somebody else, and so you put up the barriers. You're afraid of being hurt again. You've been hurt too much.

Tanya: There's something else, which might link up with how I feel about trust, I suppose. To me it's very important, and it's got a lot of ramifications. I don't actually ever believe anything that anyone tells me, not unless it's a fact I can check for myself, you know, like two and two make four. Anything that anyone says to me – even if they say 'You're beautiful', which has been said to me on occasion – I can't accept that. Love, expressions of love, praise, recognition of my work – anything like that – all the things I might think I want – I cannot believe it because I don't believe what people say. It isn't because I don't *accept* the things like the compliments or the praise, it's simply that I know very well that I can't believe what anybody tells me.

Mind you, this may be a case of flawed logic – I don't know – if I went into Edward de Bono's lateral thinking, I might find out that what I'm actually doing is thinking around corners or something. But the progression of thought seems to me to be: I can't believe what anybody tells me unless it is a fact. If they say to me: 'Your work is good', 'You are beautiful' or something like that, I ask myself: 'Is that a fact?' And since I have no evidence and can't check it for myself, I don't believe them. Deep down, I *never* believe anything anyone else tells me, unless I can check its truth for myself.

Charlotte: I can appreciate that, particularly as people mainly talk in a language that's not straightforward.

Tanya: Well, I do understand the language from the point of view of my work. I mean, I use it because it's the way that everybody talks. The language human beings use to me is completely dishonest, it's the most twisted, convoluted method of communication there is, but I understand the way it works, I use that in my books – the defences, the lies, the prevarications, the whole sub-text of speech – maybe being a writer I'm even more aware of real meanings than somebody who isn't a writer. It's a basic tool you have to get to know – to whatever degree – if you're ever going to write about people, create believable characters.

But for myself, outside of my books, I won't trust it at all. It's something I want to get away from. I do understand 'their' language, though, I can talk it, and I will do, and have done all my life. But inside, I don't accept 'their' language, and I don't accept anything that's told to me. Maybe that's why I've had to end up writing this book, since I didn't believe anything that I was told by psychiatrists and doctors, self-help books or anything like that. I didn't believe it until I tested it for myself.

Charlotte: There is a perfectly commonsensical element in all this. I mean, nobody's arrived at forty or whatever without realising that particularly in this century, with television and the massive amount of media, we are now very familiar with the lies that Big Businesses tell us, the lies that the politicians tell us, the things that are supposed to be so good for us that turn out five years later to be intensely bad both for us and the environment – let alone the church, which is almost another area altogether -. It means that fairly soon in life now, I think, the disillusion, the disbelief, the positive shock at the lengths people will go to persuade others that their product, their party, or whatever is the best, best, best, must begin to dawn, and it's perfectly understandable. With you, though, it obviously goes very much deeper, and back to the things that were said to you as a child, which were frightening but were actually demonstrably untrue, so that even as a child, you came to see they were untrue, though you were still frightened by them.

Tanya: I was frightened?

Charlotte: You were frightened by things that people said that were actually not true, and when you realised they were not true, you resented the fact that these things had hurt you, and started to keep yourself in reserve, keep yourself doubting, if you like. Unconsciously, of course, and I doubt whether it happened as clearly as that. But your not believing what people say is partly from your own experience of this and partly from what has reinforced it, particularly your work as a writer.

Tanya: Well, when people speak to me, I do know what they mean, in fact I can probably speak their language better than they can, because it's my job to juggle with words, use them, create effects – the effect I want – with them -.

Charlotte: What I was meaning was being able to recognise that people were saying one thing and meaning another.

Tanya: Oh, I can do that to. And when people say something to me and they mean something else, I know what they are doing. I don't have to trust absolutely then find I was wrong – I know exactly what they mean, and I know what they're saying is not what they're perhaps trying to say, not what they're meaning to say. I can appreciate and recognise the convolutions of meaning, I think. But it doesn't endear people to me or make me feel they are any more reliable because they use all these twisted methods of communication – protection, defence, aggression and so on, everything being covered up or hidden, or meaning something else. In a way, it gives me what probably sounds like the most conceited and arrogant feeling that I – myself – know what is honest and true, and I could if I wanted to, speak in another language which would express honesty and truth and cut out all the messing about and saying one thing when you really mean another.

You know when you listen to children talking between themselves, and an adult will say rather patronisingly: 'Well, yes, they're talking baby-talk'. That's how I feel when I listen to most adults talking. They don't know what they're saying to each other. To me, they're just babbling in what you might call 'adult baby-talk', and even though I know what's behind it all, I feel very much removed from them.

Charlotte: Boasting like children, when there's no substance to their boasting?

Tanya: In a way I regard a lot of people – most people, I suppose, whom I meet – whether this is justified, I don't know, but I regard a lot of the things they do as child-like – babyish. For one thing, people's preoccupation with something that seems increasingly prevalent these days – the sort of expensive and useless 'executive toys' – little mini-golf-courses to put on executives' desks for them to while away any spare minutes when they're not being executives -.

Charlotte: When they're being paid God knows what a minute.

Tanya: Yes, but what they're being paid doesn't seem to me to enter into it. I feel if people have got nothing better to do than play with mini-golf-courses, and they have no capabilities even to see the limitations in which they live, it's sad and rather pathetic. Sometimes, you know, I think things are the other way round to what everyone supposes. Children are 'childish' and adults are 'grown-up'. But – I don't suppose I'm the first person to say this by any means – I think maybe the way in which I was trapped or repressed or whatever in my childhood has left me with a child's way of looking at things, but a brain to think about them which has – I hope – grown up, and so I feel – or I can see – that the directness of childhood, the honesty, the refusal to accept what you know to be a 'sham', and a lot of other extremely useful and valuable qualities, have been lost along the way so far as many adults are concerned, and they haven't been replaced by anything else that's worth having.

The language I feel I want to speak – the honest and direct and truthful one I was talking about earlier on – well, that's the language I still accept, myself, as being better than all the convolutions that cover up hurt pride and outrage, shame and guilt and the sins that are forced on us with growth into our society – it's the language a child uses – and a child speaks from the heart. It's only when you've 'grown up' that you start to talk 'adult baby-talk' – and that's not from the heart, it's from your wallet or your inferior position in the hierarchy of the office, or the fact that you want to get the girl sitting on the next bar-stool into bed with you.

Charlotte: I think there's a great deal of truth in what you say, and I haven't heard it expressed quite this way before, though many of the greatest artists and writers – creative people – when they're interviewed – acknowledge that they've kept a 'child-like vision' – retained it. I don't think anyone would ever dispute that a child has a freshness of approach, a freshness of description – sees things totally unprejudiced by the sort of attitudes that prejudice adults. Our senses can definitely become dulled, language can as you say turn into a cunning weapon to achieve one's own ends – heavily camouflaged, of course -.

Tanya: I suppose this is what I was trying to say when I wrote in the manuscript about the face of love masking one's murderer, the smile hiding the dagger waiting to strike. In fact, you know, Charlotte, I think this might be a very basic thing I've been aware of in myself for a long time and tried to express without ever being able to fit it into words that made any real sense. You can often picture a feeling – like a smile hiding a dagger – without really realising what you're actually getting at – it's instinctive, intuitive -. I think this is why so often when one reads a poem or something, one will see what appears to be a very simple sentence, and then, as you said about Dannie Abse's comment earlier on, the words themselves sort of dissolve and they're bringing you a much, much deeper awareness that's being communicated through another channel altogether, a much more vital and real message.

Sometimes, I'm sure the person who wrote the words doesn't even realise all he might be conveying through them, but even Freud said somewhere that creative writers have knowledge far beyond what anyone could ever dream of, and are able to draw from sources that science and psychology and experts on the workings of the mind can't even begin to grasp. But it's an intuitive knowledge and you don't learn it, you're just sort of, well, put in touch with it, like being tuned in to a certain wave-length, and the messages come through in images or impulses in a sort of code, and you write the code down, even if you don't really know what the message is all about. But there's always – *always* – this certainty you mentioned right at the beginning of our talk, a complete and utter certainty of truth. When I wrote about the smile masking the dagger, I knew how I felt inside – very, very angry, very hurt – and I put it down as best I could. But I didn't really understand *what* I was putting down, and now I'm starting to see what seems like a glimmer of light at the end of a tunnel.

Charlotte: The directness of how a child speaks, you mean?

Tanya: Well, if one possesses this 'child-like vision', which I think I must do – although I have to admit, I've never really realised it or thought about it -.

Charlotte: You do have the freshness of approach a child has – and I mean that as a compliment, not as an insult.

Tanya: Well, what I'm trying to say is that if I do still have this vision – if I've never lost it, or I've regained it or something, that must be why I find most adults – by and large, I mean – so extremely boring to get along with, because 'talking their language' to me, is mostly a waste of time. They're not concerned with intuitive truth. Apart from the fact that a child's experience is obviously limited, a child or a person who retains this 'vision' seems to me to possess something far more valuable than what you're supposed to have as you grow older, what seems to be generally regarded as adult wisdom. I think the wisdom of the fresh, child-like approach is – to me at any rate – much more wise.

Children don't seem to have any need, generally speaking, to 'cover up', they don't say one thing when they mean another – if they're happy or sad, they say so; if they're hurting, they say so. And what's even more important – to me, at any rate – they don't take offence when somebody else does the same. They live very much closer to the truth than adults do.

Charlotte: This is why, perhaps, a group of children can be so refreshing, when a similar group of adults would be rather a depressing prospect to me, I think. A child retains its individuality in a way that adults don't. It's very difficult to take a child's individuality away from him. In view of all this – you say you don't trust adults – you despise adults – but would you trust a child?

Tanya: Yes, I think so. I might not like the child, but I would probably trust it, because generally, children are not trying to prove anything – they are basically honest in consequence. If a child said it would do something, then didn't, there'd probably be a perfectly reasonable explanation. But if an adult said it would do something, ninety-nine times out of a hundred, whether the thing got actually done would probably depend on all sorts of considerations – all of which have to be added up, sorted out, made allowance for.

Adults seem to me far more pathetic in their adulthood than children, because – well, I suppose they can't actually *learn* less, but they lose – in most cases I think, willingly and even eagerly – what they knew intuitively as a child, and all they replace it with is the sort of devious and self-defeating 'games' Eric Berne has described in *Games People Play* and his other books. A child will look at something and see it for what it is, but most adults look at a thing and they don't do this, they see it in terms of money or what it's worth as a status symbol or a projection of themselves.

Charlotte: They cover up the honesty of a child as regards their feelings, too, for the sake of being 'polite' or 'social'. Not, of course, that people who retain the 'child-like vision' necessarily retain also the childish way of spilling all their emotions out without trying to deal with them in a reasonably sensible manner.

Tanya: It strikes me that most of the time, adults are frightened to death, and they try all the while to pretend they're not. That's what all the 'executive toys' and the manipulations of language are in aid of. Children are much braver. They *are* brave. Most adults are not.

That's why, I suppose, that having had quite bad problems of my own to try and cope with myself, I've felt that the effort of having to sort out getting through to other people – supposedly normal people, I mean, not even ill people – through all the barriers they put up in order to protect themselves against goodness knows what, when all the time they're claiming they're perfectly well balanced and able to cope and know it all better than I do – I find when I *do* get to them that I have no respect for them because they're – well, often much less than what they claim to be. I always feel myself that I have to look after so-called 'normal' people – I have to be the one who makes the effort to get through to them because they're too frightened emotionally to come out to me. I feel I can communicate with people who've retained this 'vision', I suppose, and who speak 'my' language instead of 'theirs' – I have come across others who can, and when I do, I recognise them, they're – well, one of 'us', not one of 'them', in a world that's largely full of 'them'.

But once people have lost it, or more important maybe, won't admit to having anything to do with it, I see only two types of relationships I can make – one is to love them, but to take into account that I have to understand them and probably pity them for their limited vision and their hidden fears – or to use them in any way I can without actually harming them, if this seems necessary. Neither of these, of course, is anything like what love should be. I've loved a lot of people, but probably never *really* loved them in a healthy sort of manner, even though I might have sacrificed a lot for them, cared terribly, torn myself apart for them -. I don't see how there can be any two-way relationships between 'one of us' and 'one of them', whether the 'us's' mean I'm mentally ill or simply that I've retained this language, this vision, childish quality, or what. I suppose it's another double bind. I can't have a two-way relationship with someone I can't trust, and I don't trust anybody at the moment.

There's a tremendous difference between 'us' and 'them'. If – as I suppose I've tried to do for years – I have to go into 'their' world and live the way they do, I will act a part all the way through, take no notice of what anyone says, pay off any debt I incur, whether it's emotional or material, in whatever way I can – usually money, that's the language 'they' seem to understand best – and then get out as quickly as I can without becoming involved.

At the same time, though, I can see that underneath all the layers 'they' cover themselves up with, most people do still have this quality – they *could* talk 'my' language, but they're afraid of it, and they won't admit either to having it or being afraid, because in some way that would make them seem weak. And they're afraid of being weak. But the way I see it, you can only find your strengths by admitting your weaknesses. If people would do that, they'd become stronger, better, more humane, understanding, decent, than if they carry on cluttering themselves up with desperately trying to persuade everybody else how big, strong, capable, brave they are.

Charlotte: I know what you mean. Philip Gross puts it like this: "Do we grow *up*? I think we grow *out*, accreting more selves round the child in us."

Tanya: Yes, that's it absolutely. As people grow up, they seem to just load themselves up with a load of junk, around their personality, I mean, and then they go round carting it all about. I've always doubted myself, felt I was in the wrong because I didn't fit, wondered what was lacking, but maybe I was trying to judge myself by standards that to me are completely unacceptable and superficial and have nothing to do with what I see as real worth and real value. Maybe that's why I've always felt so worthless, because I was making desperate efforts to be something I didn't even want to be anyway, and even that didn't seem to be good enough. And so inside, I kept myself back, and wouldn't trust what I was told and wanted to work out everything myself, and deep down, I felt that *I* and my own judgements and opinions were the only real things I could depend on. If you can't trust what other people say, even as a child, you have to learn to depend on yourself, and what you say to yourself.

Charlotte: In 'your' language.

Tanya: You know, Charlotte, maybe the 'child-like vision', the language, has got something to do with being prepared to question, as I had learned to question, with being prepared to – well, sort of look things in the face – look the truth in the face if you like, not hide from it and squint and look the other way and try to pretend it isn't there. That's the child's directness, the child's honesty.

Charlotte: Ah, truth is another of these intangibles. Something we shouldn't try to label, I think. Or were you referring to any specific truth?

Tanya: No, I don't reckon there's any such thing as a specific truth. People have said a lot of things about it – the most famous is Pilate, of course: "What is truth?" That's generally considered to show he was less wise than Christ, but I don't think it proves that at all. The gospels were written to express the truth – or whatever – as Christ saw it, and even though the church regards his messages and his credo as the one great universal truth to end all truths, it wasn't anything of the sort, it was Christ's own truth, personal to him -.

Charlotte: And, of course, distorted by being passed on through the disciples, and so forth.

Tanya: Yes, but even if he'd actually stopped and explained what he considered his truth to Pilate, maybe it wouldn't have been anything like what Pilate needed or wanted – I mean, everyone has their own truth – Christ had his, he knew his because it was personal to him, his own – but we must all have our own, not someone else's, we have to find it for ourselves, it's something that's got to be unique to every individual -. Wilde's got a speech in *The Importance of Being Earnest* – very witty, but terribly, terribly true. 'Truth is never pure and rarely simple.' Maybe that's why so many people are so afraid of it.

6
THE KEY

Somewhere very deep down, the tightly-curled petals of a small closed flower are beginning, slowly, cautiously – very cautiously – to unfold. Just a little. Just a little.

I have two links binding me already to this strangely quiet land in which I find myself, two people I have learned during my journey to respect for their compassion and their personal strengths, their willingness to look – as I have had to do – into themselves without fear of the failings they may discover. Like me, they've made their own journeys during the writing of this book, journeys that I cannot know about but which I sense within my own mind that they have faced unswervingly. Very cautiously, I am beginning to feel I can trust them. I hope I may come to love them, but not too much yet. I don't want to have to back away.

Like me, they have both been through suffering, they have both been scarred in the past. I must respect their reticence, their right to remain – to whatever extent they choose – private individuals. Perhaps this is what I must do with everyone. Not pity the fears and the reluctance to meet those fears, but search instead for the lost and bewildered child who hides somewhere behind the barriers of defence. I have been too quick to condemn, to judge. I must learn not to storm the barriers but to wait patiently until those barriers are lowered voluntarily. I cannot force others to face their truths, it is something I must leave for them to do themselves. I must respect their dignity, their strivings, their right to find themselves their own way.

Nothing has changed, and yet everything is different. I have to get used to it, learn how to find my way around. But I'm not so unsure of my balance now, if I stand still, take things quietly, one step at a time, I feel the ground will hold me, it's not going to cave in suddenly beneath my feet. Not just now, at any rate. Maybe tomorrow – the next day – something will knock me over. But I can't hope to avoid that. If I hold onto myself, refuse to let myself go, I will find each time I fall that I become more confident I can pick myself up again. It will take time – the rest of my life. But I feel inside – I know – that this is the right way to go.

The nerviness is still there to some extent. Perhaps it always will be. I'm still hesitant, still frightened in case I prove unable to do what is required of me – but required by myself now, not by other people. Mainly though, I have found calmness of thought, peace of mind. I am no longer angry. No longer driven by devils, haunted by the shadows of old mistakes, griefs, sins. They may come back, but if they do I think I can face them and defeat them.

It wasn't so much a sudden dramatic victory I had over my illness, a final great battle from which I emerged triumphant. There have been no fireworks, nothing I would be able to use as a writer if I wanted to bring this chronicle to a climax the way it happens in books. In life the big moments pass almost without being noticed. In the words of T S Eliot, worlds end 'not with a bang but a whimper'.

I turned round ready for the fight to the death but my enemy, with whom I have struggled for so long, had become unsubstantial as mist, drifting into nothing in the rays of the morning sun. I have been striking out all my life at phantoms. To me, they were more real than my own self, but when I found myself, they began to fade, to dissolve, to linger only moments before they passed into their own unreality and ceased to exist. No sound – no word – no confrontations with guns blazing, the battle had been fought with no awareness of it on my part. In the dark hours, as I slept, they had gone. I do not think they will ever return to haunt me again.

*

The key that unlocked the door for me – the final piece of the picture I was struggling to grasp when I started to write this book, the answer I have been searching for all my life – came in a final 'revelation' from my subconscious even before my last long talks with Charlotte, but I didn't (then) realise what it was. A step forward, certainly, but it wasn't until I had talked out the remainder of the dark ghosts of old attitudes that were still troubling me, that I came to see the significance of what I had written down as it passed into my consciousness.

It is my lifeline, something I want to learn to cling to and hold onto always in this world of thought that is still so new to me. I can't try to explain it. I can't add any more to it. For me, it says everything.

'Charlotte said: "But don't you see, you don't *have* to want blue or green curtains, you don't *have* to want strong or weak tea. You are as you are, you're yourself, you don't *have* to be interested in what anyone else might be absorbed in."

'It seemed the same as what everybody else has always said – "You can't do this, you can't do that!" – which I have always so much resented. And then I saw it wasn't. Oh, the blind who will not see! Shining like a beacon, the simplest truth that I have probably read and heard hundreds of times. It's not a new thought but in my case, I have had to work it out for myself. I had to be able to reach the point where *I* could see it. The difference between "You must" and "You don't have to".

'I realise now that all through my life it has been a case of 'this is the way things are – you must accept them'. And I wouldn't accept them. I fought and fought, though vaguely aware in sick desperation that even if I succeeded in rejecting them I would be no better off. It was a classic 'double bind', no-win situation.

'"You *must* accept them," said somebody – God, I suppose. And I cried back equally relentlessly: "I will *not* accept them."

'"You must live," said God. "I won't," I screamed "I'll die." And I ended up unable to do either.

'And all the time the answer was there, but I was not able to see it. It isn't a question of "You *must* accept this." I may not want to accept it; I may still want to fight it; I may not like it. But how different, how amazingly, wonderfully different if I had realised that I actually have a choice. The alternative to "This is the way things are - I must accept them" is: "This is the way things are - I can *choose* to accept them." Even the bad things, the difficult things, the things I don't want.

'In going back to that original primitive pain, the deep hurt that was still tormenting me in the depths of my mind, I didn't have it forced on me this time. It wasn't a case of the little entity thinking, "This is hurting and I don't like it. If this is the way things are, I reject them, I don't want to know." Nor of God, or whoever, saying, "Well, you've got no choice, mate, you're stuck with it whether you like it or not!"

'But when the original pain, hurt, rejection happened, that was what I felt, and that was what I experienced when I went back. I didn't want things the way they were. I turned the other way, I fought them. And all my life I have been doing the same thing.

'If only that little entity had been able to say to itself: "Yes well, I don't like this hurt, but I suppose it's the way things are. I can't change it so I suppose I'll have to accept it for now. It might go away soon."

'When I went back, I deliberately – so far as I was able to – opened my mind to the pain. I *chose* to go back, to face it and accept it. If I *choose* to accept other seemingly unbearable and unacceptable facts, they appear far more in proportion. I don't need to torment myself with them any more. I can't alter them, I *choose* to accept their inevitability.

'I can choose to accept all the things I have been fighting against for so long. It will not change them; they cannot be changed – this is the way things are. But I can choose to accept that they cannot be altered, and I can concentrate instead on what *can* be altered to deal with them, put things right, make matters better. I couldn't alter the world, but by writing this record and going through all it involved – making my own decision to do it – I have altered myself. And found that I can choose now to accept the world as it is, myself as I am.'

TANYA BRUCE
London, October 1987.

TANYA'S DIARY

PART ONE

1
AN OBSTACLE COURSE

14 OCTOBER

Yesterday I finished The Book. I think Charlotte is worried in case I descend into depths of depression but this time, it's not half so bad as usual. I have been writing in The Book about how to learn to *want* to come out of my head into the world, so I am taking an interest in other things, making small plans, instead of drifting round lost until I can summon up the energy to plunge into work again.

I feel as though I have been very ill and am too weak to tackle much. Not physically, though I'm very tired, more mentally. I'm very feeble. Can't cope with much at a time, because I'm trying to deal with every little thing as it happens. I've got to do this or I will lose myself and have to go a long way back to find myself again.

Making the effort to 'hang on' to myself sounds harder than 'letting go', but it isn't. It's when I do let go, and forget to hang on that the tension comes. I let go without being aware of it, and started a nervous headache - was going to take painkillers, but once I had made the effort to 'hold on' to myself, the tension and the headache disappeared within a few minutes.

Tiredness is the enemy. Everything's worse when I'm tired, and I seem to have got very exhausted after a seemingly uneventful day. BUT – a letter did arrive from my literary agents, with whom I am getting terribly disillusioned. (I will in future refer to them only as the 'Regent's Park Rowers', here's why) - .

- I sent them the first part of The Book but their reaction was: to dismiss it more or less entirely and

- To detail instead their own 'terrible experiences' – eg. 'a feeling that I was going mad' and 'pangs of depression'.

Charlotte said it's as though they had met me staggering into Sydney Harbour after sailing my dinghy round the world, masts gone, sails torn away, and insisted on detailing their own awful experiences to me about when *they* rowed round Regent's Park Lake! I admit I was deeply hurt, and when *that* letter arrived, I almost gave up trying to finish The Book, or make any contact with the outside world.

This morning's letter wasn't so bad, but I can tell I have embarrassed them. They are sorry they ever read the manuscript. They would rather forget it. I understand their fear, but it still hurts, the rejection and shutting off of any attempt to comprehend – let alone consider worthy of approval, and they are my *friends* - what I have tried to do, what I am trying to say. The effort of trying to cope just with that letter and the small events of simply living have exhausted me more than a hard day's labour.

Earlier today I slept for two hours, heavily, my mind still churning on like a mechanical crusher eating up whatever is in its path, whether I want it to or not. Woke up somewhat refreshed to realise I have had at least three – four – maybe more 'manic' impulses (small ones) since I got the letter from 'Regent's Park'. *Must* do something – *now* – *now* – (involving spending on phone calls, of course). Also had a 'brilliant idea' I could have done without (more phone calls, more expense). I had stopped myself giving way by 'hanging on', but not realised until after I had slept that these were 'manic' panics. Thought of Diana's poem. Must HOLD. Always HOLD.

Don't try to rush. Keep the energy, save it for when I need it. Move forward very slowly – I'll get there faster. Be still – hold steady – don't run away with half of me before the rest of me can follow. Keep the ranks closed – that way I'm stronger. If I split my forces, I'm lost.

About my daughter. I can see she has some of the same tendencies I have had – she has distanced herself from me. I would help her if I could, especially now, with the understanding of myself that I think I've got from The Book. But *do not* give help unless she asks for it. Let her make the decision. If she needs me, she will tell me. If she doesn't trust me enough to tell me, I will only make things worse by forcing advice or help on her. She has to find her own way – she *wants* to find her own way. Let her. I am still here if she should come to me. I don't have to keep reminding her of that.

15 OCTOBER

Had a long talk with D. this morning about the 'schizoid personality'. I told him how, at thirty, I went into 'withdrawal' for eighteen months after suffering a big breakdown, and how both then and as I was coming out of it, I kept falling asleep all the time. Even visiting relatives. I couldn't help myself, I'd just go off, wherever I was. The family got rather fed up with it (not surprising), but we just accepted it as 'sleep.'

Could it have been some sign of catatonia? I have not read much on the 'schizoid personality' – never thought it had anything to do with me. Now I think it has – or had.

Seems to be characterised by polarised and/or inappropriate emotional responses. I told him how I felt nothing, deep down, for other people. All fake, all sham. The lines were always shut. No way of getting through. If D. or Charlotte cut off communications, I'd put the barrier up even now after all we've been through together. Still can't trust – only think I can at the moment. But can never be sure.

Went out to do some business errands this afternoon. I met another one of 'us'. She has had a stroke, got terrible problems but fighting bravely. Maybe 'we', 'us', are the fighters, the ones who've got to keep battling all the time. She is very fair, very honest in business dealings. I thought, yes, that proves something – she talks true.

Coming back a few hours later I felt very lonely and lost. Kept repeating my life-line – *I have accepted all this, I have* **chosen** *to accept it*. But I don't want to reach out to anybody. I don't want to go any further than Charlotte and D. yet. I lose my bearings. Too much conflicting pressure from outside me. Even the expressions on people's faces, the look in their eyes. They are all hunted, beating their way through the jungle.

Do I really want to make any contact at all? I don't think so, not yet. I am conscious now of being enclosed within myself, but I can't do anything about it. I feel very strongly that I don't want relationships.

One thing might be good though – I am talking my own language now instead of 'theirs'. Wrote a return letter to someone who has just got over mild depression. No deep down troubles, but afterwards she went back to 'their' language, started talking down, patting me verbally on the head.

I refused to write the gushing effusions of pretended friendship. Just wrote simply. I hope she doesn't write back again. I don't really want to know, don't want the drag of what she imagines friendship is, she doesn't know me.

It's not being very easy. But then even a little step further forward is something. I saw a dead cat on my way home, killed by a car. Soaked in the rain, just lying there. I forced myself to look (in case I recognised it), gave a little thought of gratitude because at least it wasn't maimed and suffering. Said to myself that I have *chosen* to accept this little cat's death. I was saddened, but not slashed to pieces inside as I would have been before The Book. Rest in peace, little cat. The world can't hurt you now.

16 OCTOBER

A night to remember! It was the night of the Great Hurricane, the worst since living memory across the south of England. D. was awake for hours in the dark, disturbed by the howling winds, collecting candles and distributing them through the flat when the electricity failed. All the street lamps went out. Total blackness. Chaos for everybody in the morning.

I slept through it all. Yesterday evening had knocked me out, so the hurricane passed over my head, as it were. I had phoned my brother – had a chat about a forthcoming family birthday, family news. It was a very strange feeling. He is a good and honest person who I think would always try to understand, but even people who are willing to try can't always grasp immensities, it isn't fair to put them to the test. To him, I am the sister he has always known. He is fond of that sister – but would he feel the same about *me*?

I think not. How can people whose patterns of living are safe and real, stable and unchanging, comprehend what it is like to have lived always, under the surface, on the edge of a snake-pit? Would they want to share my groping in the dark, my wanderings in and out of sanity?

I mentioned that I hadn't been well.

'So long as you're okay now,' he said, backing away, as it were, from the details, and I assured him that yes, I was quite all right now. What more could I say? – 'Well actually, I think I am – if not already schizophrenic – teetering on the verge, but not to worry, I have managed through a tortuous exploration of my mind to establish contact with myself, and I *might* even be able to exist *normally* one day if I try hard enough.'

If I had actually voiced the thought he would probably have responded (in a cheery manner suitable to my obvious state of lunacy): 'Well, that's all right then,' and escaped as quickly as he could to consult with the rest of the family – in genuine concern – as to whether the time had come for some kind of institution where I wouldn't have to worry my head about anything.

It must have been all those breakdowns – I mean, she always was a bit odd but she's gone right over the edge now, and after all we are her brothers, it's up to us to see she's properly taken care of - .

I was saddened. I even began to wonder whether the new reality I am trying to become familiar with was just a figment of my imagination.

Went to spend an hour with a friend. I was very tired but had promised to visit her, and staggered home afterwards with legs trembling and threatening to give way, reeling from exhaustion. Trying to 'hold on' in any social situation takes a lot of energy.

But the day wasn't over. At half-past ten, she phoned me in a highly-charged emotional state. Terrible crisis! Stray cat who recently found a home in one of the flats in this block has been shut out in the rain by his new owner, who has apparently now departed London on business.

What, demanded my friend in pitiful and trembling tones, was she to do? As a cat-lover, she had rallied to the rescue and taken Puss into her own flat out of the appalling weather but her eccentric feline had spat at the intruder and no way was going to let Puss share its place by the fire. Puss now shut temporarily in my friend's bathroom.

She waited after revealing these sordid details for my usual emotional rising to such an occasion, my offers to go across and 'help' – ie. provide an audience while she held forth at great length and to no avail about 'what could be done'. But faced with this pressure, I surprised myself by remaining calm, advising her not to panic, suggesting that Puss could spend the night in the communal hall of the flats – didn't dare to say that he could probably survive a night in the rain, that cats can make themselves comfortable in odd corners even if it's pouring, that in fact she was creating a melodrama out of nothing.

I felt this was how my new self should try to view the situation. Accept it, *choose* to accept that Puss has been fed, that he might get a bit wet but he'll live until tomorrow when owner returns. No real problem. But assuring me in tones of the utmost reproach that *she* wouldn't have been able to sleep a wink if Puss hadn't been saved from the elements, my friend said in a die-away voice that it was quite all right dear, she understood, and put the phone down.

At this point, commencement of quiverings of guilt at having failed, worry because Tanya has not done what was so obviously expected of her. The usual pattern. In the past I would have spent a sleepless night myself wrestling with inadequacy, becoming increasingly convinced that I had been somehow responsible for Puss's wetness, the owner shutting him out in the rain, the annoyance of the eccentric cat and my friend's quite genuine attack of hysteria.

In fact I felt none of these. I had somehow lost myself, and was in a state I am becoming familiar with, though I am not quite sure what it signifies - something to do with both exhaustion and an inability to accept or register any more pressures of whatever sort. It's as though my brain has been kicked into a stupor and everything – colours, noises, impressions – is trying to add another kick but I am too insensible to notice any more. Time ceases to mean anything. I am not even aware what day it is. Nothing surprises me. I long at such moments just to lie down, simply to collapse onto the floor and shut everything out. At first, for a long time, I thought that what I wanted was sleep. Now I am not so sure.

I do not think any of my sleep is 'normal' – the quiet drifting off into slumber to wake refreshed and full of energy for another day. Sometimes I cannot sleep at all, and heavy doses of drugs make no impression whatever. When things are not so bad I can, with the help of sleeping pills, manage a night's drugged oblivion but I wake heavy-eyed and lethargic, and need some time to shake off the lethargy.

That is, perhaps, the nearest to a 'normal' night's sleep that I can get. Quite a lot of the time though, I will reach the exhaustion point, or even go past it, and if I am able to lie down I need to spend some time 'bringing myself back' as it were, to the point where sleep is actually possible. In many of these cases I either plunge – whatever the time of day – into a very heavy sleep that is like dropping sheer over a cliff into blackness impenetrable, though when I wake I am aware that I have experienced long, vivid and complicated dreams; or else I seem to drift in and out of a state that is between sleep and waking, my brain whirling fragments and images madly in all directions. But even though I am not actually out of touch with consciousness, I am unable to 'wake' until my brain has finished whatever it is doing.

Both this semi-consciousness and the cliff-like drop into blackness seem to be unaffected by anything that might happen in the outside world. Last night, for instance, I plunged after reaching and passing the exhaustion point, and heard nothing of the hurricanes that must have woken everyone else in the South.

When at one stage I surfaced briefly, to be aware of a red candle flickering in the room and D. informed me that there was a terrible storm and the electricity had been cut off, I felt no surprise or wonder. If he had also imparted the information that we had had an earthquake, or a tidal wave was expected at any moment, I would have had the same total lack of amazement or interest. It's as though the deep sleep or the 'waking sleep' will not let me go until it is ready. It will not let me return to experiencing what one might call 'ordinary' reactions, or even to be concerned about my own physical survival.

In my befogged state last night, before going to sleep, I thought that recent developments – and The Book – must have been something I had dreamed up, that nothing had happened at all, that I had not changed, that I was only kidding myself I had progressed anywhere. I lost the ability to HOLD. I did not even trust myself. The bewilderment came back. If I hadn't been too tired I would have tried to write it down, this wail of: 'Where am I? What am I? What am I trying to do? And why?'

When I woke this morning it was still there. There was no self, no Tanya. No sense of time, no ability to cope at all. I wanted to just escape again into oblivion but the hurricane had drastically curtailed D.'s plans to go to the Midlands on business (partly on my behalf). Frantic phone calls had to be made. I *had* to try and cope. D. quietly let me. Gradually I felt some sense of self return and I was able to grab it and hold on, realise what time it was, what day, where I was, what I was doing.

Saga of Puss (continued)

I phoned my friend to enquire how he (and she) had survived the hurricane and the night. She, of course, had not closed an eye – had indeed spent much of the time stumbling round the garden with a torch after the electricity failed, calling to the eccentric cat which jumped out through the cat-flap. Would I go and give her moral support. New owner of Puss, it now appears, has not only shut him in the rain for the night but *will not be back for several weeks*. Puss is abandoned! Must find another home!

Once her 'audience' had arrived, my friend proceeded to phone various other people to ask their opinions – and to debate whether owner has actually gone away at all, or lies behind the locked door murdered – generally to work herself up into hysterics all over again. Solution, one of the pet protection societies perhaps, but no guarantee that Puss would not be put down if handed over to them...

I hunted out a newspaper, found advertisement for Pets' Hostel where they do not put any of the animals down but find homes for them all, eventually persuaded her to phone them instead of continuing to just mutter. Three phone calls later, Angel in Disguise promised a place for Puss at the hostel in a few days, and I agreed to undertake the journey to deliver him (in the capacity of 'stooge' to his heroic rescuer) when notified, hopefully soon.

My friend was by this time weary but triumphant. I was beginning to feel my legs quivering, my mind going into the same state of non-existence as last night. Two hours had passed! I managed to get to the door, trying to say all the right things, such as: 'Yes, it's been a terrible strain for you, just try to rest...'

When I got back, had lost all trace of self. Wandering outside time. She would never comprehend what I mean if I said I was exhausted, too exhausted to take any more today. 'How can I be more exhausted than she? I slept all night, *she* never had a wink. I kept quiet, kept calm, *she* did all the hand-wringing, the emotional acrobatics. *She* did it, I only 'helped'.'
But the only thing that really matters – Puss will have a good home. D. took some extra tins of cat-food for him. I sat down to try and 'find' myself again. It's weakness, not tiredness. Simply can't take too much pressure, knocks me right out. There is so little of me there at the moment. But couldn't let Puss down – I care about him too.

Felt exhausted this evening, at the 'exhaustion point' which I think *can't* really be exhaustion at all. Brief phone call to Charlotte, a few words. Amazing. The exhaustion just went.

I realise now that I wasn't really 'holding on' earlier – never came back to myself, perhaps, after the saga of Puss and having to communicate with my friend speaking 'their' language – all cover-ups for her own fears, her own worries, her own need to assert herself. I understand, I tried to give support – in a roundabout sort of way, 'acting' of course since she would not tolerate or accept 'my' language. But afterwards, very difficult to cope with finding myself again until Charlotte's voice brought me back.

What does this 'exhaustion' that, like the nervous headaches, can vanish when I make contact, actually mean? What is it? Very real if I have not got a proper awareness of myself. Also brings with it a sense of distance. I little while ago I sat listening while D. made some phone calls. I felt a million miles away, right off inside myself though I wanted to be close. But it was too much of an effort. I didn't really care – I didn't want to be bothered about anybody, not even D. I had no interest at all in anything. Just tiredness, space, a long, long way between myself and everybody. Now I am suddenly real again.

I wondered earlier on whether, by finding myself in The Book, becoming aware that I do exist, I would make it easier for this self to disown all contact with others. That would definitely be letting the side down – D. and Charlotte and the garrison of four-footed companions who support her at the other end of the phone. So I'm thinking of D.'s sensitivity and care for me, his gentleness and so many expressions of concern every day; thinking of Charlotte's trust and faith, her own slow and hesitant lowering of barriers, afraid of a slap even from me; thinking of her much loved pets in Cheshire lending her their clear-eyed strength in their belief (which I can only endorse) that she will not fail us -.

I swear I will try to fight it to the death, this distancing of myself from others. Not because they need me – as the excuse has always has been in the past. But because they *want* me. My God, that is such a fantastic tribute! I'll write it again. They *want* me. They love me. I have seen it in their eyes, and to me eyes speak true, say it all.

At this moment, I can feel for D.'s eyes, Charlotte's eyes, the eyes of her feline and canine troops. Yes, but nobody else's eyes, not yet…

It lasted only a few seconds though, for as long as it took to write that last sentence. Then I backed away. But surely I have achieved *something*? A *real feeling*, even if it was only for a minute. Not sham or fake, 'mania' or sentimentality. A *real feeling!*

I don't have it now. At the thought of what I was doing, I slammed all the barriers down hard. No way, I said to myself. But I'm willing their eyes to hold onto me, not to give up. I won't ask – a 'yes I will' says nothing. Theirs is the decision to make…

Even willing for them to hold onto me was too much. You can't trust anybody. If they think I want something from them, their eyes will change. Their eyes frighten me. I don't want to see any real feelings anywhere. Whatever I do, the eyes will change.

I won't look at their eyes yet. Just keep the lines of communication open, and wait.

17 OCTOBER

I have just got up, had breakfast, smoked *one* (only one) cigarette so far, and it is quarter to twelve. I have got to try and keep very quiet today, do some consolidation.

Is there no end to it? she asks despairingly. Will there ever be any end to it? Will I ever be able to relax 'holding' so hard without losing my new identity, my new reality? At this moment it all seems, as Charlotte said, very frail.

I surfaced reluctantly from the depths of sleep earlier on, back aching, head aching, eyes bleary and bloodshot, generally extremely ropy, very weary, didn't want to know about the existence of Saturday. Then I mumbled under my breath: 'Yes, I suppose I *choose* to accept all this, I'll take backache, headache, the feeling that I don't want to bother, the lot. Pile on the agony, boys, I've said I'll have it!'

Relief was, I must say, hardly evident to the naked eye. The miracle cure, my life-line, is wearing a bit thin. But then, I assure myself with gloom, it's only early days yet.

Thinking of Joanne Woodward in that old film *The Three Faces of Eve*. At the end the three 'personalities' of the disturbed heroine became fused together again into one - a wonderful acting tour-de-force for Joanne Woodward, but how did the real Eve feel afterwards, I wonder. Did she too have to 'hold' to keep those three personalities together, fight against disintegration every day with no real time or energy for anything else?

The impression one gains from that flushed and smiling woman, 'complete' at last, poised and triumphant, is that it was just a case of *snap – snap – snap* as the three personalities slotted into each other and then hooray, hooray, it's all over! I think she probably had a hard time later, woke up like me with backache, headache, too weary to want to even try to 'hang on' to herself.

Heavens, I've lost Number Two today! This won't do. Come on out, you naughty girl, where are you? I know you're there somewhere!

I wonder, Eve, whether as you grappled with yourself, you watched the film they had made about you and had a good laugh at the idea that the fusion of your three 'faces', your three personalities, was the end of the story. Off into the sunset, all problems solved. What a joke!

Since I 'discovered' my identity, however tenuous my hold on it, I am aware that I am becoming rather too big for my boots. Where is the 'formidable humility' Charlotte wrote about in The Book? Last night on the phone, I was really airing my knowledge at her, knew it all.

But it's not so funny. Can the discovery of my own personality lead me into even further nasty habits? *From Non-Existence to Megalomania and Delusions of Grandeur in 1 Easy Lesson, by Tanya!* It's a sobering thought. I will have to keep myself under control. Maybe I've learned a lot but I will never know it all. And I don't want to. I said to D. that it would be rather awful, if one knew it all. So very boring.

'Yes, it's nice to keep finding out,' he said.

My dear quiet, gentle D.! I have to admit that, though I am not as dependent as I used to be (I don't think so, anyway), on either him or Charlotte as a love/hate object, I do need them both. Without them I could not carry on, I think the institution my brothers might want to provide would be the only answer. There is something very comforting this time to feel I'm not so alone, that we are going forward together, the three of us and the 'garrison' – though our four-footed friends have no need to admit faults and compare notes with us on their difficulties!

I've never wanted be part of a team before, never really allowed myself to feel I wasn't the boss, not really, not deep down. But without them – Charlotte and D. – Tanya Bruce would be in a sorry state.

'It's a sort of feeling of cameraderie,' said D.

'Like soldiers fighting a war together,' I agreed.

I hope they feel this too. Nothing so hair-raising as loving each other – I couldn't face that yet – but that we are all heading somewhere acknowledging our dependence on each other. Already we've come a long, long way, but there's still a hard and winding road ahead.

Alone this afternoon, I was well and truly defeated by - a headache, returned from this morning with reinforcements to batter at my skull. Panic! *What is it?* I shrieked to myself, wondering frantically what portion of reality was doing what to another, for my brain to be receiving such a lot of tension and my head to be aching so badly.

All my perceptions about which was my past (wrong) reality, and which was the new calm, capable self who looked at things differently, fell in at the deep end, gulped once or twice, and sank without trace. I was left with – what? Not depression exactly, since I have voluntarily resigned the status quo which I suppose caused the depressions and the frantic 'manias', and I knew that was not the way to go, even though it was tugging at me to return to the old, familiar paths.

But I could not find any sign of my new reality. Both the old one (which I could feel pulling vainly) and the new one (which I could not regain at all) had gone. So what was left was a sort of helplessness, since I was really outside of them both. An awful feeling of doom. Incapable of doing anything at all, let alone work things out. Meanwhile, headache continued on its merry way.

The solution? I had no idea what it was. Crawled into bed, hardly able even to move, and lay doing relaxation exercises I have been taught in the past, to try and untangle the knots of panic and tension and ease my head. Eventually drifted off after working hard at relaxation, to sleep.

Woke rather warily two hours later, wondering who I was going to be when I opened my eyes – Tanya or the defeated 'self' of pre-Book days. Have tried to clarify the situation in these pages, and since I have been able to express myself calmly and am not panicked at this moment by the headache, which is still there, and am no longer a jumble of iron-hard and quivering muscles, I think I must be MYSELF (my new identity) at least to some extent.

I have taken painkillers for the headache – a sensible solution I think, instead of rushing off madly in all directions and attributing it to mental warfare. It is probably exactly what it appears to be – just a headache.

Thinking now of the talismans I armed myself with in the last chapter of The Book. Diana's poem. HOLD – and that does NOT mean grab tightly, reach out, strain forward. So, avoid pushing, trying too hard. Just hold quiet. Be still. (How many times, I wonder, will I have to tell myself this? In panic, it all goes out of the window.)

It's definitely not as easy as the moguls who solved it all for Eve would lead us to believe. Maybe in reality, she came unstuck the very next day. Ran around in three pieces for a bit until she could find them all again…

One thing seems clear. I have turned my back on my old identity – the one that has kept going for forty-three years. The temptation not to abandon it was there very much this afternoon. All the habits of the past were tugging at me, but I didn't want to give way even though I was saying to myself: *What if you've made some ghastly mistake? It's like the marriage ceremony this, you know, till death do you part! Come back, at least you know the old way worked after a fashion.*

No, I think that has gone for good, so I'm stuck now with this new Tanya, through thick and thin, richer or poorer, whether I have D. and Charlotte's support or not. It's not a thing you can do in easy stages, this, nor by halves. It's all or nothing, and I suppose I have chosen 'all', though the 'all' at present is very small, very feeble, very newly-born. The only alternative is the 'nothing' of past guilt, shame, fear and pain which I have worked so hard to be rid of. However much it beckons, I cannot – I do not want to – go back. I've got to go on. In the best way I can. With or without a headache.

Best news of the day! Since I started writing, the painkillers (or something) are working. Headache almost gone! So on we go, having hopefully learned something from this afternoon's chaos. The obstacles are so unexpected. I have to take each one as it comes. But I'm not downed yet.

2
IN PART

18 OCTOBER

Yesterday after talking to Charlotte, I shut down all communications, retreated into the far distance, became extremely depressed and decided that I would not write any more. I did not want to communicate with anyone. I would not speak. Something had reinforced my inner conviction that nobody was to be trusted, that the rose hides the thorn, the smile conceals the dagger, the friend is a foe.

That might have been the end of this diary. Nothing more to say. Gone out of time. Don't want to know. However, I managed to speak a little later to D., and in between convulsive tears told him how I felt, that I didn't want to try any more, it was too difficult. I had given up.

And then, by what miracle I do not know, the abscess burst and I was able to release the poison inside, which I think is what has been bothering me for the last few days, the cause of all the depressions and uncertainties. I was, of course, completely unaware that anything *was* bothering me until I managed to drag it out and talk to D.

It is so pathetic, so small a thing and yet to me, of such immense importance that it has completely incapacitated me mentally for the last few days. It is: *The question of my agreeing to accompany my friend to take Puss to the Pets' Hostel* -- I had reacted to the fact that my friend had unconsciously used exactly the same methods of coercion to get me to agree to go with her, that have been responsible for my helplessness and resentment – and anger – in the past.

It seems as though whatever my mind has decided about identifying my 'real' self, and however hard I try to 'hold', there is something inside me that responds to a certain type of pressure in exactly the same way it has always done, instinctively, without my being able to do anything to stop it. I end up in all such cases in a 'double bind' unable to act rationally, unable to move in any direction, filled with frustration and rage that expresses itself in desperation and withdrawal.

IF I CAN IDENTIFY THIS PATTERN AND BECOME AWARE OF IT, I WILL PERHAPS BE ABLE TO BREAK 'DOUBLE BINDS' MORE EASILY!

To an ordinary person it is all so simple. 'Tell her that you won't go,' was the obvious answer to my dilemma. Yet I quite literally *cannot do this*. The mental effort involved in saying 'I will not come with you' is to me so tremendous – impossible, in fact – that the pain and desolation of depression and withdrawal are infinitely more preferable.

BUT! Last night I actually managed to break this 'double bind'. I said to D. that, looking at the situation sensibly, I had several choices.

- Offer to take Puss on my own? (Unacceptable to my friend, who wanted the glory of rescuing him herself).

- Tell her I was unable to accompany her? (Would, I felt, provoke the reaction that I had let both her and Puss down badly and ought to be ashamed of myself, an attitude that in the past has been fraught with guilt and shame and made me suffer agonies of spirit).

In the end I decided that I would phone to tell her I would not go, but since I didn't want to be punished by having my concern for Puss denied to me, I would independently send a donation on Puss's behalf to the Pets' Hostel. After which decision had been reached, I knew I had broken the 'double bind' but was so exhausted from the effort that I collapsed in the state that follows intense demands being made on my mental resources, where I find it very difficult to move, think, do anything.

This morning, when I came to make the phone call and spoke in my new 'Tanya voice' of calm, I discovered that, as might well have happened so often in the past if I had ever been able to try and break 'double binds' – a thing I have never been able to do before – all my agony had not been necessary. Since I did not immediately plunge into defensive/apologetic confrontation and make an issue of it, she casually mentioned that she would probably take Puss to the Pets' Hostel on her own – just like that.

In effect, I have been excused. Now, I feel I can *choose* if I wish to offer to go with her, and I will feel no resentment, no anger, no pressure, no coercion. I will probably go if she asks me now, because I will have been able to make the decision for myself. But if she uses the same tactics that put me in this 'double bind' of the last few days, I will want to refuse, and have to cope with it all over again.

I feel it is important for me to explain this situation fully, as I am certain it will be completely incomprehensible to most people. They will not be able to envisage a grown woman who is literally incapable of saying 'No' when pressured to do something. But anyone who has ever experienced the mental torment and phenomenal effort of trying to break a 'double bind' will understand only too well.

It is this way, when through emotional blackmail and subtle but cruel force so vicious that the personality on the receiving end is – as I am – unable to trust anyone, to believe anyone, wishes to shut down all forms of communication with others, feels nothing inside – it is this way that true madness lies. Not just a small case of 'nerves' but a complete blanking out of self, an absence of all desire to have anything at all to do with other people.

With me, the lines of communication are still, mercifully open. But if I was to be subjected to the form of pressure that puts me in 'double binds' for any length of time now, I know I would retreat, cut off, shut down. And, unlike depressive illness where the patient feels a terrible desire to communicate, a person who has withdrawn into himself or herself has no wish to communicate or be communicated with. There is no (conscious, at any rate) desire to unburden oneself to a concerned and compassionate listener. Every expression of sympathy, anxiety, love, willingness to help, falls on ears that are not deaf, but cannot accept them, since they know love can in a moment turn to hate, concern to blame, sympathy to indifference.

'I am your friend,' says the voice.

There is no evidence of this. It's just words. Ignore it, turn the other way. Silence is the best defence, since whatever I say will be twisted and used against me. Let them know nothing, that way they cannot harm me. Or, if I speak, babble irrelevancies, but do not under any circumstances reveal the truth.

While I was writing The Book, I deliberately refrained from consulting psychological texts as I felt it was necessary to record as honestly as I could what I really felt, and if I had 'read up' in any way, I might have tried to fit my symptoms into patterns, which would have distorted the true picture. But after I finished The Book I did look up certain subjects in Charles Rycroft's *Critical Dictionary of Psychoanalysis*.

I know this is not a wise thing to do, but since I have been forced by circumstances into being – so far as I can – my own analyst, I thought I might be able to distance myself enough to try and use the information sensibly. Apply it, as it were, to the evidence in The Book, much of which I have never before been aware of consciously. If I must help myself, I would be foolish to ignore anything that might assist me to understand what I am trying to do.

19 OCTOBER

At Euston Station, drinking coffee. Came with D. to see him off on business day in the Midlands – the business that was interrupted by the hurricane. Still quite early – not yet half past ten.

Woke this morning struggling against a very odd feeling. It isn't depression or withdrawal, panic or building up of 'mania', though some tension, just a little. More of an awareness, which I felt very much coming here on the Underground and as I sit in the station buffet, of being absolutely *on my own* now – relying on myself.

The prospect of standing on my own two feet is horrifying in its immensity. I am quivering inside, but surely things can only get better? I'll get used to it. I've *got* to get used to it. I *have* to learn to manage for myself, not be a parasite on someone else.

Poor little Tanya! I thought with an inward sob of self-pity, then gave myself a kick. *Shut up, you coward, and get on with it. You've got a long way to go, start moving!*

It has dawned on me since yesterday that (putting on one side consideration of depression and 'mania', which I decided to leave alone after realising from the *Dictionary of Psychoanalysis* how very involved it all was), I do have a splitting of my personality. I think that cannot be disputed.

I said during the long phone conversations I held with Charlotte while I was writing The Book, that it was as though the vices and the virtues had become separate units in me. They have not split so entirely that I am not conscious of them, but I do feel that the 'good' part is the 'real' me, and the 'bad' part is someone I hate and don't want to acknowledge.

106

This, I understand, is fairly common in illness like mine. Both of them – certainly in my case – are extreme attitudes. My 'good' part is too good to be true; my 'bad' part is, in my eyes, utterly despicable and awful. Whichever part of me is in control, I cannot help but over-react to an alarming degree.

This must, of course, be stopped. I have to try and bring my two selves together, steer a course of moderation, recognise that I am neither very good nor very bad, but a bit of each. I think the new personality I have become aware of since writing The Book is probably in the early stages of composing itself into a fusion of the two 'old' selves, but I am not sure yet. It's too soon to know. I have not got used to the new Tanya. She isn't accustomed to existing, she is finding everything very bewildering and strange, extremely tiring and wearing.

Had an odd thought late last night. With the realisation that I had split into two selves at some unspecified time in the past – probably early on as a result of the 'double binds' into which my mother unconsciously drove me - I saw that my whole life has been viewed independently by each 'self'. In fact, I looked through the pages of my autobiography, which I wrote last year, and suddenly realised that to gain anything like a true picture of Tanya Bruce, it would be necessary to read both the autobio and The Book.

Without in any way being aware of what I was doing, I wrote my autobio with my 'good' self – it was a perfectly sincere and honest account of relatively happy and successful times so far as my 'good' self is concerned. But I wrote The Book about the dark, the years of mental suffering and pain, with my 'bad' self, possibly assisted by Tanya Number Three, my brain, which has detached and is, I think, trying to stand back from them both. So even though the two books, while chronicling the same life – my life – see my years of living from different viewpoints and appear to be incompatible in that the feelings and emotions they express are entirely opposite, each was written in all sincerity but by warring elements in my personality. Each is therefore, so far as it goes, a truthful account.

I think it will be just as bad for me to continue to live on a deep, questing mental plane as it was when I tried to repress my conflicts and 'be good'. Neither is right for living. I had to come down from an airy-fairyland into the depths, but I must not stay in the depths for ever. I must again aim for a middle course, an awareness of both, without going to either extreme. I have to bring both the heights and the depths into focus together – only then will I be able to develop this new identity, this new self, and achieve real balance and peace of mind.

12.40 pm. I have spent the last hour or so talking to two sisters. It knocked all the self-righteousness out of me. Quietly but smartly dressed, discreetly made-up, they queried whether the other places at the table where I was writing in the buffet were taken, and with the openness of people from small towns where everyone is a potential friend and not a stranger, began to talk as they settled themselves with cups of tea.

Their names were Vera and Joan. They had travelled from Nuneaton, and after chatting for a few minutes about how lost they felt in London – they have only visited a few times before and find it frightening, such terrible pressure, a whole different way of life to their own – they told me Vera is going into Barts Hospital today for an operation on her eye. It is cancer, and she knows she has only a fifty-fifty chance of surviving even if the operation is followed by radiation treatment.

'I'll feel better after Thursday, when they've done the biopsies,' Joan told me simply. 'At least then, it'll be definite one way or the other. We'll be able to try and accept it, whether it's good or bad. We've got to. If you can accept things, it makes all the difference, doesn't it? It's the not knowing that's so awful.'

Vera was unbelievably and valiantly bright-faced. She spoke little of herself, but was more worried about her husband and daughters, whom she had left at home.

'He looked so lost on the platform – he would have cried after the train went. I couldn't bear to wave,' she said reluctantly, adding a little later: 'I'm not so much afraid of being dead. It's having to leave them behind to cope. He keeps saying: *You're not going to die and leave me*, but that's refusing to face facts, isn't it? I mean, you get past the tears and the crying and the protests of 'Why me?' Why *not* me?'

I felt hopelessly inadequate, and simply listened. It seemed to help them to talk - they lost their mother a few months ago, nursing her to the end, and now *this*.

'It should have been me, I have no responsibilities,' Joan said. 'Vera's got her husband and daughters, they'll be devastated if anything happens to her. Though I feel like I'm taking my own child to the hospital and handing her over. She's my baby sister, we've always been close…'

For an hour we sat sharing a table. Three women, the bustle of life going on around them, talking quietly. Nothing so special about that, yet we were matter-of-factly, steadily sharing the prospect that for one of us, there might be no tomorrow.

I did not try to utter reassurances we would all know were false.

'You're going in fighting,' I told them. 'And that's everything. You've accepted, but you haven't given up.'

Vera grinned only slightly shakily.

'I'll go on fighting to the end. I don't want to die. I mean, life is so good, isn't it?'

On my way home, I bought a card and posted it to the hospital. I will phone tomorrow after the operation, to see how she is. Whatever the outcome, I know they'll face it with the same dignity, the same gallantry.

'I'm not the bravest of people,' Vera said, and Joan smiled a bit crookedly.

'By the end of the week, I think I'm going to be the one who'll need to go into hospital!'

Dear Vera, dear Joan, you are two of the biggest bloody liars I have ever met!

All I could do as they picked up their cases and prepared to go was to wish them luck. But for what it's worth, I shall be thinking too of the surgeon's knife tomorrow, willing him to bring Vera through the operation safely. The rest is out of all our hands.

21 OCTOBER

Yesterday I wrote nothing except a few scrawled notes. I had to make some important decisions to do with my work – the mundane facts of earning my living, keeping solvent. Had to make phone calls, write letters, but trying to assert myself in the world 'out there' still takes a tremendous effort, leaves me drained and shaking.

The situation is continuing to clarify itself more and more. I have identified that there are actually three separate parts of my personality in operation at the moment – perhaps some digging about under hypnosis would reveal more, but so far as I am concerned, three is quite enough to cope with at present. Two are the 'selves' I became aware of earlier - the 'good' girl and the 'bad' girl. The third has definitely emerged as an unfeeling, logical brain, which sometimes dominates me so that I have no emotional responses at all, I simply deal with working things out – though in an extremely efficient manner, I admit. But 'the Brain' (or Tanya Number Three), is just as unpleasant as the other two if it takes over entirely.

I scribbled the following note yesterday evening, when I was tired, thinking I was talking about my whole new self. I can see this morning that I was really describing 'the Brain'.

'I am finding it difficult to know myself now. My brain is coolly and logically coping. It is so unfamiliar that I am half-afraid of myself. I see everything differently – I do things in ways that seem strange to me. I feel lost in an odd sort of manner without the inner pain, the consciousness of keeping myself apart, the fear. Tanya's calmness, her efficiency, her methods, are very intimidating, difficult to come to terms with. I do not know whether I really like her or not.'

Sometimes, especially in the mornings when I am relatively fresh, I manage to get the three of them more or less working together – some 'brain power', some feeling, a steadiness and balance that gives me the impression that I am (so far as I can be yet) a reasonably normal human being, not just a lost little girl or a wild creature bent on having its own way at all costs, or even solely an efficient and rational thinker. But without being aware of it, I slide over the edge of the slippery slope during the course of the day, and can go from one part of me to another without knowing where I am, as they draw further apart.

Tiredness and effort will send me over the edge and break up the happy entirety. I have not yet managed to have a whole day as a complete personality. It's something I am working for. What a day that will be!

I cannot describe the tremendous upheaval taking place in my life and in the life of D., who is the closest to me. We didn't ask for this stunning and unbelievable thing to happen but now that it has, we must follow it through. The impact has been rather like being struck by lightning – it isn't exactly the easiest situation to cope with when one changes into a completely different person, or at least, is in the process of that change. We have no rules to follow, no guidelines. No-one with whom we can compare notes.

(So how did you manage, Doctor, when you turned into Mr. Hyde..?)

I would very much like to be able to discuss the proper procedure for turning into someone else – quite literally – with the real Eve of the Three Faces. It is hardly the sort of thing one imagines will ever happen to oneself. I have to learn a whole set of new emotions, new outlooks, new reactions. I have to become familiar with myself. At the moment, I feel as though I am walking around with three people trailing behind me, holding hands. *Come on Number Two, don't hang about, try to keep up with the others...*

One thing I do know though. When something of this nature begins to happen, it is impossible to stop it progressing to the bitter end. I don't think that at any time during the writing of The Book or what has followed, I would have been able to say to myself: No, I've had enough, I'm going no further. It is like a landslide, you just can't call a halt halfway through, you are swept along until you reach the bottom and the debris settles.

Maybe it is a miracle. But if it is, all I can say is that miracles are far more complicated than people think, and are very uncomfortable and tiring. A lot of people who wish for miracles would be scared into headlong flight if their miracle actually happened. One's whole existence is completely turned upside down. Something has hit us, that's for sure, and we can only try to hold onto each other until we discover where it is all going to end.

I am so very thankful that D. – and Charlotte – had the courage to accompany me along the way without backing out. Experiencing a miracle alone would be, I am certain, too much for any living person. Even if I do actually end up 'cured', the cure has been many times more traumatic than the illness has ever been, or ever could be. There are established paths along which you can tread in illness or even in misery – with miracles you are uprooted and completely out of your depth, and you also know that nothing, absolutely *nothing at all,* will ever be the same again.

News Flashes

Phoned Barts last night but Vera had not yet had her operation. It is this afternoon – about now. The nurse who spoke to me from her ward was young, fresh, had a soft Scots voice that vibrated with life. Vera is in good hands.

I wish a miracle for her this afternoon, she wants so much to live she will gladly accept all the discomfort.

Second news flash came yesterday. My friend phoned to say that Puss has found a new home. Another resident here at the flats has taken him in, though she already has one cat, a queenly female who did not get a chance to express her feelings towards the intruder, since Puss – who is obvious regaining his confidence – spat at her first!

Yesterday evening, Puss and 'Queenie' were sitting at opposite ends of the room, a truce declared. Whether either was brooding on the best method of attack for this morning, I don't know, but there have been no further reports of hostilities. I hope he's settled for good this time.

The impossibility of what has happened keeps sweeping over me. I phoned a business colleague early yesterday, mentioned diffidently that I had discovered I was really several people and was now in the process of trying to put them together. He was actually shaving at the time, and how many men would be able to take that sort of talk when they were doing something so prosaic as shaving?

He seemed to accept the whole affair quite matter-of-factly. But I can't help thinking that most other people I know would find the concept incomprehensible. It just does not happen, especially to one's relatives or friends.

As we have progressed through the events of The Book – the 'descent into the depths', for instance, and my wavering in and out of time and reality, my sliding about into the different parts of myself – we have become very much aware that when apparently unbelievable things happen, they don't announce themselves with a roll of drums so that everyone can gasp in wonder. They simply occur, and take place so quietly that you *don't* gasp and say: 'My God, what a fantastic occurrence!' You just accept that they have happened, and that is that.

Although it does not seem very comfortable to me to be split into pieces, it is at present a way of life, and we (D., Charlotte and I) accept it as such. It has happened, it is there, we live with it. I suppose the moral is that you can get accustomed to anything.

Tonight I took what I think must be a terrific step forward. I identified the early stages of a 'double bind' and managed to break it without any help from anyone. All on my own, I did it! Three cheers for Tanya!

I did not, of course, realise what it was at first. Depression set in – the effects of 'double binds' always seem to be worse at the end of the day, maybe because my resources are lowered. I think they have always worked like this, unless I am being subjected to the kind of pressure that causes them constantly, when the effects are ever-present.

But on some occasions in the past (mainly late at night, or even in the middle of the night), I have found myself so driven that I have felt unable to remain in any room in the house, and have in a traumatised state removed myself from communal living and huddled, depressed and withdrawn, in the loo. The paralysis induced held me immobile until I was either forcibly dragged back or reassured that I was welcome to share the fireside.

The sense of alienation, rejection and worthlessness induced by a 'double bind' is indescribable. You know you are not wanted. You are riddled with guilt because you feel you owe an immense debt to the person who has rejected you, but since you are paralysed with helplessness and sick depression, you will never be able to do anything to pay off the debt. You cannot move in any direction, you stand exposed, like a butterfly on the end of a pin, knowing that whatever you do will only make matters worse. Being aware that the people who have rejected you have problems of their own makes you even more sorry for them, but increases your own sense of worthlessness and inadequacy.

I could never break 'double binds' in the past since I did not know they were there, and the people around me could not shake off their own torments enough to help me. But tonight I was consciously aware of that familiar ache of lostness, isolation, misery. Tanya – my new self – was nowhere in evidence. *Maybe she'll come back in the morning,* I thought. *I'm just tired, that's what it is, tired and very tense.* And then somewhere, a bell rang in my head.

I felt like this the other day, and it was all because of a 'double bind' – wasn't it?

Thinking isn't easy in the clutches of depression, but the more I tried to identify the feeling, the more convinced I became that something was bothering me, something I had got to sort out. I mentally sifted back through the events of the past few days and emerged, like a diver surfacing with a pearl in his hand, with the root of the trouble.

I have mentioned the 'Regent's Park Rowers' (my agents), who have in previous letters squashed my efforts at trust and communication flat, told me instead about the 'terrible' problems *they* have had to deal with. They do not want to acknowledge what has happened to me, they do not want to know 'Tanya Bruce'. But because of various business decisions I have made today and acted on, I am due to receive (perhaps tomorrow) some further communication from them. The letter is almost certain to express annoyance at my personal interference in matters which they consider should be left to them.

Naughty girl, they will scold, *when you know we know what's best for you, we are amazed and deeply hurt at what you have done without consulting us...*

The way that 'double binds' work becomes clearer each time one of them occurs. What I am actually so afraid of is nothing overt – often there is no real threat at all. What causes my distress are the METHODS employed to put the message across which can automatically activate those oh-so-familiar reactions in me - reproach, blame, the inference that I have no say in the matter, that I had no right to take action, that by doing so I have wounded everyone else to the heart and made things extra difficult for them...

...and goodness knows, we have enough to cope with already, trying to take care of your business affairs; you should be humbly grateful – instead, you've really put your foot in it this time – caused a lot of extra trouble - you should be ashamed of yourself - etc, etc...

The actual facts of any particular situation – even the actual contents of the letter I shall no doubt receive in due course - do not enter into it. Tonight I was going into a 'double bind' because, from experience, I was *expecting and anticipating* the pressures that would provoke my own involuntary reactions of anger, terror, panic and helplessness. The smile hiding the dagger, the friend who turns inexplicably into a foe, the denial of my own rights and the imposing of the rights of others.

People who induce 'double binds' always employ the same methods, and because of their own inability to face up – think deeply – consider implications – because they are afraid of finding weakness in themselves, their methods never change.

It is the way in which they protect themselves, their defence, and they have no idea of the harm they can do.

But maybe I can face the recriminations that will surely come (and which I do not now intend to accept humbly, admitting guilt where there is none) and cope with them. Having broken my 'double bind' tonight, I have once more regained myself.

3
THE TROUBLE WITH NUMBER TWO

22 OCTOBER

This morning we had trouble with the 'bad' girl, who was very much alive and kicking when I woke. Panic, shaking, sick misery – and most of all, the consciousness that I was short of money, that there was no cheque about to arrive in the near future, all of which ominously heralded the appearance of a 'mania'. In the past I would probably have rushed out and frantically spent what little there was left, reducing myself to a stony broke condition. Then, aware that I was now in desperate straits indeed, I would have sunk into overwhelming guilt and depression.

I managed, however, to realise today that this sort of thing simply would not do. Tanya is not going to give way to 'manias' so easily. With some effort, I calmed myself down, resisted the temptation to rush out and spend what is left in the bank, and feel as though I have scored a great victory!!!

I think perhaps it is wrong of me to call Numbers One and Two the 'good' girl and the 'bad' girl. This is misleading. The 'good' part of me was the child who tried very hard to do the right thing but could never please, and consequently carried round that awful load of guilt and failure. The 'bad' part seems to have been (though I was still rather in the dark about her until I was able to consider her activities this morning) a flinging away of all responsibilities, restrictions and attempts to please, and indulging in some kind of frenzy – most often a frenzy of spending.

Strangely, these 'spending jags' do not seem to happen when the money is there in large amounts, but when the money is running short. It is as though Number Two says to herself: 'I am running short, so I had better spend what I can now, as I won't have any to spend at all once it has gone.' The fact that this course of action will only lead deeper into trouble has no effect on the panic pressure that in the past has led me to spend.

Difficulty in coping with money is, I believe, very common in cases of manic-depression (Manic-Depressive Psychosis), where during 'manias', the patient will spend extremely large amounts and even run up immense debts. It is with terrible difficulty that in the past I have been able to avoid the temptation to plunge myself into debt, and the only reason I can actually envisage why one has to make money is to pay off what relatively small debts are incurred.

If I have no debts at all to pay off, I do not know what to do with the money I earn. Large amounts in the bank bewilder and bother me. It seems as though it is not right for me to own money – I feel a terrific pressure to give it to someone. But once the money is gone, the 'mania' rears its head again and I panic because I will not have enough for my needs. I become frantically worried because it is not there, and scratch around in desperation to get hold of some – *now – at once – this minute!*

I will look round for possessions I can sell, dispose of everything and yet once I have funds again, return to the state of discomfort where I feel it is wrong for me to have so much and want to give that away too. I suppose this is another version of a 'double bind'. If I have the money I am not right. If I don't have it, I am also in the wrong.

If I am truly honest, I have to admit that I am (so far anyway, I do not know whether I can learn to handle things more sensibly) completely unable to cope in this respect. In pre-'Book' days I might well have been quite capable of reducing myself and anyone who gave me a free hand with their finances to penury. It is a shocking thing to have to own up to, but since I am trying to free myself of crippling guilt and shame in order to look my problems in the face and deal with them, I must add that I do not believe my inability to understand money is entirely due to my own carelessness or thoughtlessness.

In fact, I don't think the fault is mine at all though I have always taken the responsibility and the blame if I have spent too much, even though the 'self' who ran out and did the spending was being driven uncontrollably and I was unable to stop her. The guilt afterwards, the misery, the sick despair, the shame, would reduce me to nothing.

It was as though I was expected to cope without being given the right equipment to do so – as though I was, perhaps, turfed out on a planet where there was some sort of currency involving bits of tin that meant nothing to me, and I was never told how the system worked, what slots to put the bits of tin in, what I could expect in return, or why everyone else walked around with their bits of tin on their heads, occasionally throwing them up into the air and by some miraculous way producing more.

I think the bewilderment I feel about money stems from the same ambivalence that persuaded me that a friend could turn into a foe, that a smile hides a dagger, that if I do what I have been told is right, I will inexplicably turn out to be wrong. One has to learn to cope, and if you are being given two opposing sets of instructions when you are trying to learn, you can never know how to proceed.

- One the one hand, I feel that I was told catagorically: YOU ARE NOT ALLOWED TO MAKE DECISIONS.

YOU ARE INCAPABLE. THEY WILL ALL BE MADE FOR YOU.

- But on the other hand I was also told: DON'T ASK ME TO MAKE UP YOUR MIND FOR YOU, I HAVE ENOUGH PROBLEMS OF MY OWN. YOU WILL HAVE TO DO IT YOURSELF.

- And when, perhaps, I hesitantly tried to reach a decision – of whatever sort – the first voice screamed:

- YOU SHOULDN'T HAVE DONE THAT, YOU KNOW YOU ARE INCAPABLE. NOW LOOK WHAT A MESS YOU'VE GOT US ALL INTO!

- But if I obeyed the first voice and did nothing, the second voice would thunder: WELL, WHAT ARE YOU WAITING FOR? YOU'RE SUPPOSED TO BE IN CHARGE, STOP BEING SO LAZY AND IRRESPONSIBLE. I CAN'T DECIDE WHAT YOU WANT TO DO, YOU'LL HAVE TO WORK IT OUT FOR YOURSELF!

- If I did so, and made some further effort, however, I knew I would once again be in the wrong, and back would come the refrain from the first voice.

- YOU WERE TOLD QUITE CATAGORICALLY THAT YOU WERE NEVER, EVER TO MAKE DECISIONS. DO AS YOU'RE TOLD. YOU'RE HOPELESS. CAN'T YOU EVER GET ANYTHING RIGHT?

It is obvious that this sort of brain-washing throughout childhood robs the developing personality of any ability whatsoever to try and think for itself.

If one responded 'normally', I imagine one would say something like: 'Well, just a minute. You keep changing your tune, you keep telling me things that contradict each other. Which do you actually mean? I can't do both.'

This in fact is what I expect 'ordinary' people do if they find themselves in some similar situation. I know they will also express quite a substantial amount of anger because they are being messed about and they resent it. Maybe I too will learn how to stand up for myself now, without getting too upset. A little clarification, that's all one asks.

But if you are a child, completely dependent on your parent/s as I was, and the process has been going on since before you can remember, you are crushed, guiltily aware that you have no right to answer the voice of authority back, that by protesting you merely add to the burdens your parent is already carrying by proving that you are just as wicked and disobedient as everyone suspected. As I did, you keep silent.

Your only way of defending yourself is to admit, if necessary, that you are wrong – whether you are or not - accept the guilt and shame that is piled on your head and withdraw mentally from the battle. You cannot fight, since you will always lose. You are trapped from then on in 'double binds' until you either relinquish all interest in what the voice of authority says and mentally turn away from the world, or you learn somehow to free yourself.

I was expected to protect and defend others, but I was not allowed to protect and defend myself. My own life was effectively denied me, but I was made to see clearly that while my *feelings counted for nothing and no-one was bothered whether* I *was unhappy, miserable, distressed – or what I felt – I was expected to assume direct responsibility for any hurts of which other people complained. I had to take care of* them, *remember how sensitive* they *were, what awful difficulties* they *were struggling with, what a terrible life* they *were having.*

I want to write down that I consider I was most cruelly and criminally treated, and I don't care a damn about anyone else's sensitivity, suffering, hurt. I do not care at this moment. I am very angry. I feel I have every right to be angry. I could not say this for forty-three years but I am saying it now. I am bloody furious.

I think the fact that I managed to survive in whatever state is entirely due to my own efforts, that the world has done nothing for me, and the rest of the human race can go and hang themselves so far as I am concerned, they can starve and suffer and go through agonies, and I couldn't care less. What little I have now I have earned, not only without the help of anyone else, but in spite of everyone else!

I owe nobody anything. I was robbed and denied and treated callously and unfairly. I have suffered years of misery in atonement for things for which I was in no way to blame. I was thrown out, discarded, had sentence passed on me by people who not only had no right to pass sentence, but who I now reject with the utmost scorn.

My anger will not affect the rest of humanity, nations are not going to tremble because of my fury. But at least I have after all these years, gained enough confidence in myself to say: So I wasn't good enough, not up to your standards? Well, I don't care any more what you *think. I know I'm not only as good as, but way ahead of, the rest of you put together!*

You took your own weaknesses out on me – *I'm* the one who's won now, *I'm* so strong I don't have to take anything out on anybody! I owe you nothing, I'm under no obligations. I'll choose for myself what I want to give, and to whom, nobody's going to blackmail me or make demands on me any more...*

Late Night News

Phoned the hospital this afternoon, spoke to both Vera and Joan. The operation, which took three hours, went well and the doctors think they have managed to remove all traces of the cancer, though of course they cannot be sure yet. Vera is going home tomorrow.

Spent a few hours this evening with fellow resident who has given Puss a home. She is supposed to be laid up – though you'd never guess it as she bustled around making me a cup of coffee – with a slipped disc. Puss has laid claim to the draining board in the kitchen, where he now spends most of his time sleeping on a folded blanket. He has taken over Moira's flat, taken over Moira.

She has bought him a basket which he has graciously condescended to accept, stocked up a cupboard with tins of food, purchased some mysterious powder for run-down and vitamin-less cats to build him up. He has been starved, abandoned. We think – after conferring while admiringly staring at him while he slept – he was probably thrown out after a fond owner either removed to hospital or died, and left to fend for himself.

He is still painfully thin, though Moira is constantly opening tins – he started his third while I was there. Also may be suffering from some kidney ailment, as he has a habit of sneaking into the bathroom to try and drink out of the loo, apart from consuming gallons of milk and water from his new bowl. He is going to visit the vet on Saturday. If he needs to take medication for the rest of his natural, said Moira, he will have it. This may not be too long, as he is, we think, quite elderly, has lost all his bottom teeth.

After a very pleasant evening's conversation, took a last look at him curled up in the kitchen.

'I hope people won't think I *don't allow him* into the living-room,' Moira worried. He is brushed, groomed, fed and watered, has chosen his own place (even though the fact that he occupies the draining-board means washing-up is practically impossible). He is adjusting to the fact that he is no longer alone in the cold, unwanted and starving.

Who could treat an elderly, loving animal like that? But Moira's clear eyes have given me back faith in human nature. Puss was right to trust. I watched her lovingly and neatly straightening his tail, and he just as lovingly kept twitching it crooked again in his sleep.

Sad phone call from Charlotte very late tonight. Not that *she* would own it, still as steady as ever.

'Two happy things, I'm glad,' she said after she had asked for the latest news about Vera, and about Puss. She went on to tell me that yesterday she lost a dear friend from leukaemia after he had fought through a year on other people's blood. And as if that was not bad enough, she has had news that her sister is entering into the last stages of living with cancer – it has reached her brain. No prospects but coma, a merciful release. We have been sharing the bulletins about her sister all through writing The Book. Now the end is in sight.

Charlotte asks for no pity, having to cope with her own problems as well as shouldering such heavy losses. I could only listen, unable to find words to try and comfort her.

I think the world takes people like Charlotte for granted, Her courage, her strength, her apparent toughness never fails. It would only be if she actually broke down that anyone would be surprised. They accept that she will cope, she will not give way, she will face whatever comes with her characteristic wry smile and masterly understatement, reducing grief, loss, death, to nothing. People like Charlotte guard weaker spirits and quietly wrestle with dragons, emerging apparently unscathed to provide comfort and consolation for the frightened and the trembling.

But in their own frightened and trembling moments, who do they turn to? What can I offer her, only the fact that in spite of my reluctance to want to trust, to care, at this moment I *do* care. I don't want her to have to suffer alone if I can share the shadow of those dragons in some way, strike a few blows for her. When the beacon is failing, when the light is burning dim, even a candle can maybe help a little, and my candle is burning as tall as it can for you now, my very dear Charlotte.

23 OCTOBER

This morning I was quietly advised by D. to slow down.

'It looks like you're going into a 'mania',' he said.

I am indeed, though nothing to do with spending, more to do with making the money I feel so desperately that I need. I suppose 'manias' can take different forms, or at least, the manic energy can. I have been rushing out so madly into the world, accomplished so much work in the last few days that it is almost impossible to stop.

I can hardly sit still for more than a few moments. *The clock is surely wrong. At least half an hour gone, but only two minutes have passed…Another hour, yet it says only five minutes…*

The energy shakes me all through, it will not rest. I have to slow down, to HOLD. Don't rush, don't panic. Take things easy. Rest. Relax. If not, I will become exhausted. In fact, when I make the effort to control myself, the exhaustion is there already. I am very tired, but in the 'mania' I could have gone on at high speed all day, faster and faster, until I would long since have passed the point where I was able to sleep.

In view of the traumas and tragedies of others that have happened over this last week, my own problems seem trivial. What problems have I got? I am not – I don't think – dying. I am not suffering from some agonising disease. But I have lost myself, I have not been able to keep track of who I am. I don't know whether I am my new self, or one of the Numbers who has stealthily taken over. Certainly I am not Tanya this morning.

I think I am a Number which can do nothing but plunge wildly forward as though in a river, being whirled along through the rapids or over a waterfall, unable to catch hold of anything. The 'manias' gather force as they go, they start quite quietly, then pick up speed until without being aware of it, I am doing things I had no intention of doing, acting blindly without thought, convinced I am carrying out brilliant ideas.

I use this diary to try and sort myself out as I write, hold myself together. I am back-tracking now, remembering that I told myself very early on in these pages to move forward slowly, keep my forces together…

They have been flung apart, and I must I think try to avoid confrontations with the world for a while, even though I seem to be sailing confidently and capably through them. It's all right until you hit a rock, but by then it is too late, the 'mania' simply stops dead, sinks, and what is left is a battered and exhausted piece of wreckage.

The trouble with a 'mania' is that it will not listen to anyone who tries to tell it to slow down. *Aren't you trying to do too much?* people ask. *Not at all,* says the 'mania' confidently, *I can do all this and more – loads of things, and I can do them all – oh, don't* fuss, *it's simply that you are so slow and I am so much quicker!* But I have learned now to trust not only Charlotte but D. – though sometimes I can feel myself trying to turn a blind eye (or ear, rather) – to suggestions that I ought to rest.

In the past, the frustration whenever anyone stood in the way of a 'mania' was maddening. I would have no patience. *I* will *do it, I* will*, nobody is going to stop me,* I would scream inside. Now I try to see if there is any truth in what D. says, instead of taking the attitude that everyone but myself is a moron who simply cannot see the obvious. It is often myself who cannot see the obvious. But especially if a 'mania' has really managed to take hold, any comment which seems to be placing an obstacle in the way of what I want to get or do – even a mild suggestion that I might tire myself out, made in concern – smacks of impertinence at another person daring to interfere in *my* affairs. The 'mania' always knows best. It will brook no crossing. It will squash argument flat, shut its ears to reason, meet – if necessary – force with force. It will fight with any weapon it can against whatever or whoever seems to be threatening it.

This morning, however, I trusted D. enough to make an effort and listen to him, think the matter over. I feel now that I have written the manic energy out, and I am tired and aware of myself existing in several dismal pieces.

Don't cry, Number One, you have tried very hard and been really good – and you didn't *do the wrong thing. Number Two got on top of all of us today, and you know what she's like when she gets the bit between her teeth. I don't know why we put up with her.*

Number Three, that was a wonderful piece of logical thinking. You've sorted everything out but don't get too *carried away. We all belong together, you know, even though you are so brilliant.*

This is your captain speaking. I'm here again, I'm at the controls. It was only an air pocket, you didn't have to panic and try to bale out. Get back in your seats please, put on your safety belts. The Tanya *is still airborne, and I need you all. Come on, crew, back to work. There's a long flight ahead of us.*

Phoned Charlotte this evening. The news is very bad, her sister much worse. It may only be a matter of hours and she is standing by for a call at any time of the day or night, ready to drop everything to make the two-hundred-mile dash. Her sister is mercifully in no pain, no distress, very heavily drugged. We must hope that the struggles are over now and when her passing comes it will be easy. She is a devout Christian, and I wish for her the consolation of her beliefs, the assurance that she is going home.

To Charlotte and her family, the sad and painful aftermath of death, the heart-breaking task of trying to tidy up and file away the many small belongings which will soon belong to no-one, the evidence that someone existed physically and has been blotted out. There is nothing I can do to help her carry the burden of her loss. She wrote to me a few weeks ago when we were writing The Book, when the dark clouds were gathering ominously on her horizon, a brave and steady letter where there was no apparent sign of the strain she has been under for the past year. But the last sentence spoke volumes. *'The sun is shining!!'*

Dear Charlotte, I know that it must seem at this time as though the sun has gone out. But it is still shining, and until the day comes when you can look up again and see it, perhaps our little candles – D.'s and mine – will help to guide you safely through the shadows.

24 OCTOBER

Having been able to identify my three wayward passengers on board the *Tanya*, I feel that I am in a much stronger position to try and get them all working together. It is very difficult to say to yourself: 'I am in a mania. I have got to get out of it.' But now that I know the 'manias' are due to the activities of Number Two, the 'bad' girl, I can distance myself from her with the two other parts of my personality and address her directly – in this diary, at least. Each time Number One or Number Two (or even Number Three, 'the Brain') steps out of line now, I become a little more familiar with them. I am learning to know them and recognise them – also learning how to talk to them and hopefully stop them getting out of hand.

Undeterred by the fact that I managed to get her away from the controls yesterday, Number Two has been very busy this morning trying to take charge again, working up another burst of manic energy. She is thoroughly unpleasant. Not only does she rack me with shaking tension that screams madly for action – any action – *now* – *this second* – in order to try and alleviate the pressure of the 'mania', but she takes over my reactions to others, and my speech patterns.

This morning she was impatient, uncaring while D. was talking, she moves at such a fantastic speed that everyone else gets left miles behind. While they are thinking something out, she is twenty thought processes ahead and quivering with frustration because everyone else is so *slow*. When she has the upper hand I hardly speak, since it does not seem worth backtracking through nineteen thought processes to recall what everyone else is actually still saying. When I do speak, it is in clipped, curt tones, with as few words as possible.

She also blots out any realisation of what is going on around me. I forget – or am not aware of – chores I intended to do, things concerning other people. She rushes off on a course of action that is extremely narrow, ignoring everything and everyone else completely.

I was aware of her activities this morning, but sorting her out and dragging her away from the controls, shoving her back in her seat, is something I cannot do unless I have time alone with my thoughts, time to concentrate all my efforts without being distracted. I cannot yet make any attempt to cope with a Number that has got out of hand while someone is talking to me or while I have to pay attention to anything else.

It isn't an easy task. They struggle, they drain me, they bring on headaches and increased tension. I have to engage them in a running battle that often takes some time and leaves me very tired. The most I can do until I am left alone is to be aware of them and try to curb them – not to allow them to get worse, and not to give way.

At present I can only talk to them in this diary as I 'write everything out'. I cannot stand in the middle of the room and say: 'Number Two, you're being really obnoxious today. You're not the boss, so sit down and shut up.' That does not work. But as I write, I bring in the other parts of my personality to try and discover what is causing one of the Numbers to run riot. I have found there is usually a reason, so as I type I try to bring everyone together to discuss it in my mind.

Number Two is still hanging on grimly at the moment. She will not go away, will not give up trying to take charge until I find out what the panic is all about, so I must identify what it is. There are two reasons it might be, both lurking at the back of my consciousness. One is the fact that I have made arrangements to see my daughter, necessitating a trip to the Midlands. The other is the fact that Christmas is looming threateningly over the horizon.

Calling in Number Three ('the Brain'), I deduce that to me, there is very much of an element of 'double bind' in both of these prospects, and I think it must be nearly always the pressure of 'double binds' which drives me into either crippling guilt or manic efforts to escape. Neither Number One nor Number Two can respond in a rational or logical manner if they feel they are threatened. Since I managed to find myself, I have been learning how to assert that self, how to make my own decisions. But even the faintest sniff of a 'double bind' seems to send me over the edge, recalling echoes of that awful conflicting Voice of Authority – *'You MUST!'* and yet *'You CAN'T!'* – which obliterate any chance of being able to decide for myself.

I feel *obliged* to make the trip to see my daughter, though I know deep down I do not really want to go. Not that I don't want to see her, but I do not want to travel to the Midlands, and I don't feel at the moment up to facing her own strong and determined personality, which in the past I have encouraged perhaps at the expense of my own. I want to have a say in matters myself. I do not want to have to go along with her wishes always, putting my own desires last so that I just trail along in her wake.

…Number Two is relaxing her hold. I have got it, or at least, part of it. The tension is easing, I can feel the strain going. It seems so very simple now. If I don't want to do anything my daughter suggests, I simply say no. But at present – especially since she is not aware of what has been happening to me over the last few weeks, and I don't think I could explain, not yet – I don't feel I am strong enough mentally to cope with asserting myself over perhaps a weekend. So – I will make up my own mind. I will not make the trip to the Midlands, since there is *no obligation* for me to do so. If my daughter is disappointed, she can come to London to see me…

It is always me *who makes journeys, enquires what would be convenient for everyone else, puts myself to a lot of trouble, feels guilty if I 'let them down'. I am a bloody mug! I have always been a mug! Even if I love people (as I love my daughter, though she has not been through the traumas of The Book and my realisation that I trusted and believed no-one, my efforts to come to terms, and I will have to establish a new and different relationship with her) – but even if I love people, to whatever degree, I* still *do not owe them anything. I do not have to deny myself the right to make up my own mind simply because I must fit in with what they want. I do not have to torment myself with guilt because I have 'let them down'. I am not a piece of furniture to be moved round as others dictate. I am* me. *I am Tanya, I am myself. I can choose, I can decide, and I* will.

Number Two sitting down in her seat now, the tension has left me. I am back at the controls but writing all this has taken me three or four hours of hard and concentrated effort. Strangely, I do not feel half so tired once I have won as I do while I am struggling with one of the Numbers. Then, I sometimes get so exhausted that I am tempted to give up the struggle, but I can tell when I am in control again. There is an absence of strain, a lifting of what seemed to be blinkers in my mind. I realise suddenly that chain-smoking and endless cups of coffee and inward strife is not the only existence there is…I recall that this is Saturday, that other people are doing other things, that the world is wider than the confines of my head. I can stop now. Battle over.

This is your captain speaking. You all did very well – (I have to keep telling them that, I suppose, they are so easily hurt, so easily made anxious) *– and I am proud of all of you. You're going to make a great crew once we've got a proper routine going. But don't keep trying so hard to cope with everything on your own. Remember that I'm in charge, try and refer things to me in future. If we all get together, we can deal with whatever problems might turn up. Don't worry so much. Don't panic. You're not alone any more. I'm here. I'll be here all the time. I won't let you be hurt or upset again…*

Could not contact Charlotte tonight. Phoned her home, was told she was called to her sister in the early hours, so while I was still sleeping this morning she was already on her way. She is with her sister now, out of my reach.

I am thinking of them, Charlotte sitting maybe in a dimly-lit room, holding her sister's hand. And the drugged and bewildered spirit that is about to step across the barrier from what we know as life, into the beyond of which none of us can possess any certain knowledge, however fervently we might believe. The nurses, the doctors, going quietly about the duties we cannot cope with when faced with terrible trauma. Even, in my mind, the faithful little 'garrison' of four-footed friends who, though they cannot know the facts, must surely be aware that Charlotte was distressed and heavily burdened when she left them.

I am trying to hold onto them all, prepared, if they will accept it, to give what strength I can. I hope Charlotte can feel my love reaching out to her, my thoughts. I hope her sister's mind is eased, that she knows deep down that, so far as it is possible, she has companions along her path. She is not alone, but if she must be alone, if she must go alone, there are strengths of love and care being offered should she need to fortify her own. We can do no more.

But surely, surely there is strength we do not comprehend in human love, human caring? We will not know – since she will never be able to tell us once she has crossed the barrier – whether it made any difference. But for the sake of everyone who is left bereaved when a loved one dies – for my own sake since my mother and my husband went – for Charlotte' sake – we must comfort ourselves that in some way, the fact that we loved them, that we went with them as far as we could, kept the pacts of human commitment unbroken. We kept faith, we did our best.

The tears are for ourselves, for our own loss. They are bitter tears and must be shed in order to heal our pain. But I do not believe any more that the dead require us to weep for them, for their miseries, their sufferings, their sorrows. I still do not know where my husband is, where Charlotte's sister will go, whether things are all right. But I said to Charlotte the other day that one thing I feel certain of now, is that whatever comes after death, it *will not* and *cannot* be more difficult than living. So for the dead, wherever they are, I am convinced the worst is over, the struggles at an end, the storms calmed. Why should we weep for that?

EDITOR: Tanya's husband had died August, 1986, her mother 3 years previously.

4

THE WAY THINGS ARE

25 OCTOBER

This last week, especially the struggles with Number Two, has left me thoroughly exhausted. Slept for a good ten hours last night, woke feeling utterly drained. It would be very difficult to explain to anyone – my daughter, for instance – that I cannot at present consider myself 'well'. I am not exactly ill, not in the way people understand illness, but I think I have been much sicker in mind than I imagined, very, very sick indeed.

If this diary had been chronicling the aftermath of a big operation, or attempts to cope with a severe physical illness – pneumonia, say – no doubt I would be recording that my family had been sending cards and flowers, arrangements were being made for me to recuperate by the sea, friends were all expressing their concern and offering help while I got myself back on my feet, regained my strength.

'Sit down,' people would say. 'You're not right yet, you know they told you to take it easy for at least six weeks.'

Even if I had been able to say I had been in a mental hospital and that the doctors considered I had gone through an awful ordeal, and must have time to recover, everyone would accept this dictum, since the Voices of Authority had spoken.

'Yes, well, we don't know quite what it was – they didn't *say* schizophrenia – but some kind of split personality, and that's serious, you know…No, she's all right, quite normal now, but we have to make allowances – She seems okay really, just a bit moody…

'Oh, no, not dangerous – mind you, you never know with this kind of thing. It's very difficult for us, we're afraid to say *anything*, just in case. She does have a sort of wild look in her eyes sometimes, and she practically *snapped my head off* when I mentioned that she was doing a bit too much yesterday. You don't know where you are, really - .'

I feel as though I have, in finding myself, somehow cut off all connections with relatives and friends who knew me two months ago. I am a different person – I am Tanya now – and I have only been living in this world for a few weeks. I have to learn to know people whom I might have known all my life, all over again. I even have to decide whether I really *want* to know them. And they will have to decide whether they want to know me.

So far, in 'this' life, I have come to know only two people – Charlotte and D. – they have accepted Tanya, and Tanya has accepted them. I have learned to trust them both, and I think I am learning to love them. No love/hate objects, I love them now for themselves, and because I value them and respect them and *want* to love them.

The only other contacts I have had as myself – my new self – are the ones I have described in these pages. Vera and Joan encountered me as Tanya, though possibly a Tanya who was struggling. Whatever name I gave them (my legal one), it was really Tanya to whom they spoke.

The residents of the flats – my friend of the eccentric cat; Moira – do not realise, but whatever communications they have with me now will be on my part, the assessment of a new acquaintance. Whatever relationship existed in the past, it was with a person who does not exist any longer, and if any new relationship is to be established, it will have to be between them and Tanya.

136

The business associates, relatives and friends who have occasionally rung, knowing nothing of what has happened, ask for me by my 'old' name. I know this means they expect the 'old' me to answer them, and I have felt tempted to say more than once: 'Sorry, she doesn't live here any more. She's gone.'

To me it is perfectly natural that since I have changed within my mind into someone other than the person I have been for the last forty-three years, there should be a tremendous difference. I see things differently, I think differently, I probably behave differently, speak differently.

It was a tremendous and cataclysmic occurrence. The repercussions will also be tremendous and cataclysmic. Of course, I am going to have a problem explaining what has occurred and how it occurred to all the friends, relatives and associates of the 'old' me, who understandably will find the whole thing unbelievable. People *do not* change into other people, and if they do, I imagine that an ordinary mind, a normal mind – a mind that has not drifted into the depths or in and out of reality, but has its own routine of living firmly and clearly established – will suspect that far from struggling to sanity, I have in fact quietly turned into a raving lunatic. They will be made distinctly uncomfortable, possibly even find the prospect frightening. I think that this problem – which I had no idea I would ever have to cope with, since before the events of The Book it would have been just as incomprehensible to me as well as everyone else – is best dealt with as quietly as possible.

I probably do not need to explain what has happened to anyone. People with whom I zealously drove myself to 'keep in touch' because I felt that if I didn't I would be 'letting them down' can, since my 'old' self is no longer here, simply be left to take their own initiative. It is up to them to renew the relationship if they care to, and as Tanya, maybe I can, without their awareness, tactfully make any necessary adjustments myself.

I must remember that it would be cruel of me to force anyone to try and face up to comprehending the dimensions of time and space which I have experienced – and which, though painful at the time, seemed as I have explained earlier, to take place just as ordinarily as moving from one room into another – when it is outside the normal experience of people I know. My mother used to say that she did not like to even try to contemplate the infinity of the astronomical heavens. It frightened her to talk about infinity – really upset her. And probably the people I know would be similarly upset if I imposed my experiences within my mind onto them and insisted that they had got to make an effort to *see* what had happened.

Maybe my experiences will be of use if a person would like to know what happened, what it felt and feels like, but I cannot risk forcing the knowledge on anyone else unless they ask for it. I might have been tempted to 'tell all' to my daughter or a close friend, but I can see that it would be wrong of me to do so. I will have to handle the whole thing very quietly. If I have gained any knowledge or strength from what has occurred, I have also accepted responsibility for it, and I must take that responsibility seriously.

Inevitably during the course of The Book and afterwards, Charlotte and D. and I began to talk about incidents where the impossible seemed to have happened in other ways. Charlotte described one occasion where 'phantom' voices intruded inexplicably onto her recording for the radio of a conversation she had taped with a psychic healer.

'I *know* it happened, whatever anyone else might think,' she said.

The healer did not find it unusual, but many of her colleagues took the attitude that she had had some sort of aberration. Others were prompted to investigate the paranormal themselves, but apparently found they were unable to cope with what they unearthed, and dropped the whole thing, refusing afterwards to speak about it.

I added a contribution. I *know* that my first husband and I saw two objects which would commonly be described as UFOs when we were still in our teens and were proceeding unsuspectingly with a Saturday afternoon's shopping. They did not look like 'flying saucers', but whatever they were they did not respond to normal physical laws, such as the law of gravity, and when we had ruled out all possibilities of delusions, reflected lights, balloons, etc., we were forced to conclude that they were not of this world. We tried to report our 'sighting', but nobody seemed interested in it.

D. produced a tape recording of a TV programme about reincarnation, and we listened as the subjects detailed their 'past lives' under hypnosis. Charlotte also has a tape of a similar nature. We wondered whether, under hypnosis, I would go back further than the 'descent into the depths' which I achieved on my own and described in The Book.

But that was not a life at all, not as we understand living. It was simply an awareness of indescribable physical agony. My feeling, however, is that whether I would go into past lives or not does not really matter. The prospect holds no fears, but past lives, whether my own or anyone else's seem to me to hold as little relevance to *now* as the clothes one might have worn last year, and which have been discarded.

I said to Charlotte that I feel no surprise, though, at hearing of paranormal happenings since so much that is outside of normal experience seems to have happened to me during the writing of The Book. You cannot 'look for' happenings of this nature, they come to you, but when they come, from whatever dimension, whether they can be proved to be a genuine haunting or reincarnation or whatever, or have to be dismissed as something unconsciously created by the mind, they will happen as simply and unsurprisingly as though a friend dropped in for tea.

26 OCTOBER

I thought yesterday that I had got the Numbers all in order, it was relatively peaceful and there was no tension, no pressure. I have taken no extra drug for the last few days to calm agitation or sick shaking, and yesterday I was able to cut down my cigarettes drastically. I know I will feel better if I can do this, but when I am out of control, I am unable to make an effort of will.

I should have known better than to think it was going to be as easy as that, however. I am learning that if Numbers One and Two are quiet (no guilt, shame, worry, 'mania') then Number Three, 'the Brain', is inclined to feel that some sort of display of strength is called for, and proceeds majestically to the controls, attempting to steer me into realms of thought where I am having revelatory insights as in The Book, at such a rate that I cannot record them quickly enough.

I feel then that it is vital I must write them down and absorb them, and if I had given way to Number Three, would have been typing up my new discoveries all yesterday evening, though I was very tired and needed to rest. I managed to see the danger signal, however, told Number Three that I didn't want any more brilliant ideas or revelations unearthed for the present, thank you very much, and determinedly spent two hours listening to music - and sewing.

It is not often that I am able to achieve enough of my equilibrium to be able to actually sit and relax with something as innocuous as sewing. My 'new' life is very limited so far, and apart from going out to do small errands and what I can manage of cooking, keeping the routine going, I cannot tackle any larger undertakings like re-organising my files or plunging into a wild social life – indeed, any social life at all. I am currently a sort of semi-hermit, concentrating mostly on the problems with my three passengers on the *Tanya* and recording it all in this diary.

In the past, I suppose I 'escaped' into my work because reality was too unbearable, but now I hope I am using my writing skills and the hours I spend at the typewriter not to escape, but to bring me nearer to the world, to help me to learn not to turn my back and run away.

It occurred to me that I seem to have been writing about experiences in other dimensions and outside time and space, with what must seem like a complete certainty I am right, and there is no other point of view.

Many people might quite justifiably feel, and psychiatrists might say, that my certainty would be just as blinding if I was in fact truly 'mad' and was experiencing hallucinations in which I completely believed. *All of this* could be the chronicle of a demented brain utterly removed in a world of its own – interesting, maybe, but bearing no relevance to reality - so I have no right to put forward my experiences or beliefs as though offering any sort of contribution to rational thought or experience.

But I have not sailed through these pages convinced of my own omnipotent status, certain that what I say is right. I do not know whether what I say is right, all I can say is that since in the past I found I could never believe what anyone said (even God; he promised 'Ask and ye shall receive, seek and ye shall find; all who call on the name of the Lord shall be saved', but when I asked, sought, called on his name in the depths of misery and despair, there was no answer for me), I have had to help myself and work things out my own way. In all humility, I feel I suppose that since my experiences have helped me towards peace, they may help others.

So very many people in the world are longing, as I was, for peace within themselves. I felt there could never be any peace, now I see that perhaps it is a possibility.

I am aware that many 'mad' people are utterly convinced that their bizarre experiences are real. In my case, I can only trust my own inner feelings of 'rightness' and the sense that though I may not fully understand, things are nevertheless proceeding in the right direction. I have suffered from certain types of hallucination – or whatever one calls it – in the course of my various stages of illness, and it seems to me that when these occur, they bring with them not a feeling of 'rightness', but a great deal of confusion, bewilderment, worry and distress. You do not know what is happening. You are afraid of what may happen next. You seem to have no say in the matter.

But all through The Book and what has happened afterwards, I have, though continuing to question and doubt – often to doubt my own sanity – been aware of what Charlotte expressed as the conviction that this, however painful, is *true*. There is something about it that bears a stamp, a hallmark, that is genuine. And with this comes not worry, distress, fear, but – to degrees which are slight at first, but seem to increase as time goes on – there is an easing of pain, relief from bewilderment, reassurance.

When I felt I was slipping out of reality into my head, there was no sense of peace at all. The depression and the misery, the desolation and the despair, swamped me like deep water. But by accepting the fact that I am split into pieces and I must put these pieces together, that I am very sick but hopefully am proceeding in the direction of getting well, even though my methods might be rather unorthodox (I have never heard exactly how one is supposed to deal with fragments of one's personality when they are all split apart), I am increasingly finding that things seem to be making sense – to me, at any rate, if not to anyone else.

142

I think it is the same with what Charlotte, D. and I were discussing about the paranormal. If you can accustom yourself to the fact that there are other dimensions, treat them matter-of-factly not as great mysteries which are frightening because they are unknown, you find an immense inner calm.

We are only mortal, we cannot know or understand everything, but we agreed between the three of us that, in our own limited experience of 'phantom' voices, UFOs, my 'descent into the depths' to a place I could not comprehend or begin to describe, the possibility of reincarnation – there is a complete certainty of truth. And to me, at least, the knowledge – sketchy though it is – of other dimensions and the revelation of the fact that mortality and the life we know in this world is by no means the whole story, have brought me – strangely, I suppose – a great deal of comfort.

I do not need to ask frantically why I am here now, where I am going, what it is all about. I have glimpsed that there are immensities far beyond my understanding or comprehension, and I have realised that I do not *have* to know why I am here, where I am going, what it is all about.

There is no need for me to know. I am not expected to know. I do not have to try to work it out any more, there is a right way for everything to happen, and if we accept that we are limited by our human state, our human condition, that we can only achieve what we are capable of achieving, that we can only struggle as far as we can, then a good deal of fear and dread of the unknown, of tomorrow, of the future, will be lifted from us.

I cannot explain this in any more detail, but I think consciousness of truth, of the 'rightness' of things, lays peace like a balm, removes fear, gives strength, brings tranquillity.

I think it will be obvious that as I write, as each day progresses, I am making discoveries and having all the time to discard attitudes and outlooks. Not only the ones I must have held for the last forty years, but the ones I might have felt were right only a week, or a day, ago. I had to completely rid myself of all the old methods of dealing with life – they brought nothing but misery, and looking back now, I wonder how on earth I ever managed to survive for forty-three years, trapped in 'double binds' and eternal guilt and shame.

It seems as though I had to remove myself completely from the 'old' life, in the process over-reacting with anger and hate which had got to be expressed before I could try to make any effort to come to terms with starting afresh. I had to reject everyone and everything before I could begin to learn – in any way at all – how to find my way not back, but forward, how to try to learn to trust and to love.

Even yesterday evening I felt – whether rightly or wrongly – that D. had cut off communications with me, that he was talking in 'their' language and 'playing word games', ignoring what I said and the little wishes I expressed, imposing his will with no concern for my feelings. Straight away, I could feel myself withdrawing, cutting off.

I had the same sick feeling of fury I have experienced so often in the past, the same shaking and nausea, the slamming down of all the barriers.

That's it! I knew I was wrong to believe he cared about me. I knew I was wrong to think I could trust what he said. Don't trust anyone at all! Nobody! They'll stab you in the back even while they look straight into your eyes and assure you that they love you. Right, well now I know. Finish. I hate them all. End of story.

I was too tired to try and make any effort to get through last night, and when I woke this morning the anger, the hate, the resentment, were still there. I did not want to listen to anything D. said, I shut my ears. I didn't want to hold any communication with him at all, nothing. But I knew that I had got to bring my feelings into the open, otherwise they would stay with me, tearing me apart, making me sick and weak, and I tried to explain what had happened. It was not that I blamed him for anything, it was nobody's fault, it is the old mechanism going – rather rustily now, I hope, but automatically – into action.

I have never been able to trust anyone for forty years. It is hardly surprising that I cannot achieve this happy state overnight. But I knew that I would be unable to do anything except exist in misery unless I could clear the matter up. Once I had said how I felt, said I wanted to get over it and put it right, once I sensed the lines were open again, I was able to push the sickness and weakness away, the anger dissolved. The effort necessitated taking a Valium to calm me down, but after that I managed to sit and type these pages and recover.

EDITOR: Tanya had freed herself of her addiction to Valium, but on occasion if she needed it, took 2mg as prescribed by her doctor.

I try not to be too much of a burden to D. who is, as will be obvious, a person of remarkable understanding – for which thank God or whoever – but I am trying as hard as I can, and if there are set-backs I need a certain amount of help to cope with them. Perhaps I have learned a lot already in that I will allow myself now to ask for the help I so desperately require, and gratefully – though I hope not crawlingly – accept it, from D. or Charlotte, at any rate, though not (I suspect) from anyone else yet. I do not trust anyone else enough even to ask.

I can see that obstacles may at any time arise in front of me from all sorts of sources – my difficulties are not confined solely to keeping my three passengers in order. In dealing with them, I may perhaps be able to try and control extremities of mood, keep depression, anger, guilt at bay, curb the 'manias'. But as I said to Charlotte, I think I also have to try and overcome the other twisted and warped elements in myself.

I have to *want* to be a part of the world that consists of 'them', I have to *want* to learn to trust, maybe learn to love. I have to convince myself that I do not need to step warily, always fearing that a friend will prove to be a foe, that someone may turn on me even in the fondest moment and do me harm, that the animals in the jungle are not dangerous, that I can find a place among them. So far, I have made some progress in learning to trust and love Charlotte and D., but perhaps that is because they have come with me through the writing of The Book and have given me evidence that I am of value to them, that they care. In forty years, I have *known* by the evidence I was given that I was useless, valueless, that there was no place for me in the world. I have *known* that words of love would inevitably be accompanied by deeds that rubbed them out. Actions speak louder to me than words.

Now I am beginning to feel that at least I matter to myself, that I have some right to exist. But I do not suppose for a moment that I can say: 'Well, all right world, I'm ready to have another try, it's up to you to *prove* that you want me.' I know very well that the world would take no notice at all of this startling challenge.

(*My God, yes, we can't afford to let Tanya go, we need her desperately. We've got to show her just how much we want her, really persuade her to trust us...*)

The world does not care whether Tanya Bruce lives or dies. It is not going to go out of its way to be kind to her. I am just as likely to be 'mugged' as any other woman who walks down a street alone. The animals are still thundering around in the undergrowth, voices are still saying 'Yes' and meaning 'No'.

I can see no reason why I should persuade myself that I really want to trust. I suppose this is something that will take a long time. I do not know what the answer is. Maybe I will never really be able to completely trust at all.

One thing I have discovered is that all the numbers, especially the Brain, are completely lacking in a sense of humour. When I am in control I can tell all is well because I am able to smile and see the ridiculousness of my situation.

I'm certain that somebody somewhere is having a good laugh at the sight of Tanya blundering along in her shaky little craft, wobbling through air pockets with her three passengers clinging on grimly and shutting their eyes against the prospect of the crash that seems inevitable. I think it's one big joke myself. If you can see the funny side, things are never so bad as all that.

Maybe somehow, the ability to laugh at myself – genuinely laugh and say: 'Come on you three, never mind hiding under your seats, you're supposed to be my crew, get crewing for me, we'll make it into the Red Arrows if it kills us' – will be what will save me. Maybe if I can do that and try to face the world with a smile and the feeling that everybody else is doing the same – careering along in their own oddly-shaped planes and balloons and flying machines trying to get good enough to join the Red Arrows when really, we all know it's next to hopeless – maybe the smile and the willingness to join in the general mess will help to get rid of all the fear.

Maybe I'll learn to trust those funny little machines somehow, and stop thinking they're fighter planes that are going to open fire on me. Well, I can but try.

5
OPENING THE GATES

27 OCTOBER

Achieved a little equilibrium today, worked on a new project that has come up. But tonight, felt once again how selfish I am being dwelling on my own problems.

I have been thinking these last few days of Charlotte and her sister, wondering what was happening. Managed to get the phone number of the place where they are – a nursing home – and phoned, though reluctant to intrude on what is inevitably a family time when outsiders only add extra problems, even though well-meant.

Charlotte is bearing up, her sister still lingering, though very weak with hardly strength to talk. She received the Last Sacrament a few days ago, seemed to drift away, woke to ask, 'Have I died?' Rallied and decided she would not die just yet, but the end could come any time.

Charlotte said: 'If you are awake in the small hours, think of me.' She will be sitting through the night at her sister's bedside. It is getting late now, and I am thinking as hard as I can, dear Charlotte, trying to share your vigil. I am trying to hold you, hold your sister in my mind - .

I feel so inadequate. What can one do except offer care, offer love, offer to try and share the pain, knowing all the time that personal grief is something that must be suffered alone? She asks me only to think of her. I can do no more, but I am thinking of you both.

After speaking to Charlotte, I had a phone call from Joan. Vera is not recovering properly from her operation. In great pain, very sick and weak. Joan is bringing her back to Barts on Friday, she may have to stay for radiation treatment. They know no-one in London and since Joan is not able to be with her all the time if she has to stay in hospital for several weeks she asked whether I could possibly visit her sister, let her phone me if she would like to talk to someone.

How can I say I am not needed in the world? It was such a small thing for her to ask – to visit the hospital, answer the phone, talk to Vera. I was humbled at the thought that my presence, my voice, might make a difference. Thank God – or someone – I can get backwards and forwards to the hospital, have my sight and the use of my legs, have the phone here so that Vera need not feel alone. And thank God – or someone – that I have managed to pull my selves together enough to be able to help instead of having to cling to others myself.

'It seems strange – we only met you once, but we feel so close to you – we love you,' Joan said.

It has been as though the world *did* turn round this evening and say to me: 'We want you with us, Tanya.' I can't say any more about it, whatever I said would be trite.

But I will try to do all I can to make things a little more bearable for Vera and Joan; out of their distress, their worry, their suffering, they have given me something more precious than gold, an assurance that I am valued for myself, that they want me because I am *me*. They have faith in a stranger they spoke to for an hour, they trust her. If, in their great time of need, they are able to trust someone who might have slapped them down, laughed in their faces, how can I not strive all I can to do the same?

Joan said it was a miracle they met me at Euston, but if there was a miracle, it has been in what they have done for me, not the small things I might – I hope humbly – be able to do for them. I can't do much, can't share Vera's pain or Joan's worry. But if they want me, I can at least be there.

28 OCTOBER

Woke up this morning in the grip of a 'mania'. World had retreated, nothing there but the pressure to *do – do – do* – and do it now or else - !!! The terror mounts...

Tried to sit quietly and get a grip on myself. I have managed to calm down a little, refrained from making wild and frantic phone calls to everyone I can think of, tried to concentrate on talking to D. about everyday things. I told him I was sorry I was so snappy, explained that I was trying to HOLD. Trying to concentrate on anything is an effort. I cannot bear ordinary conversation, want to scream and smash everything in sight if I can't rush off and do whatever the 'mania' has decided it must do.

Quite a lot of the time, the 'mania' seems to be connected with communications – I feel I *must* try to communicate, try to get through, and I will phone anyone just to gabble the words out of me, release the tension. I think Number Two is roused into action if she feels communications have been cut off, a sort of desperation since no-one is there – no letters, no-one talking to me, no-one exists, the world outside has shut me out and I am banging frantically on the gates screaming:

'You can't do this to me! Let me in! Let me in! Listen, you've got to listen! I'm here! I'm outside, you shut the gates and left me outside all on my own! *Listen to me!*

I think Number Two has been banging on the gates of the world for a very long time. I can never remember when I was not shut out, when the gates were not there. Even as a young child the same fury of rejection, the same panic to try and make somebody hear – *Listen! Can't you hear me? Can* nobody *hear me?* - has driven me in quivering and terrible anguish to try and batter down those gates.

It is difficult, even now, to believe that my shrieks may be provoking a response, that somebody may actually be drawing the bolts. But I don't think it would be very satisfactory if I left Number Two to handle the situation. She will never be able to see that the gates might actually be opening, she would not believe it.

I feel in myself – my new self – that there is no need to scream out my anger, my frustration, my isolation any more. If I keep still, if I HOLD, not only will the gates open, but perhaps, as has happened with Charlotte and D., Joan and Vera, the world will come out to *me* and say, as it stumbles through the barriers which no longer exist:

'Thank goodness you heard me, Tanya. I have been calling and calling, I've been so alone, I was so frightened out there. Thank goodness you opened the gates. I am so glad to see you, so glad you're here!'

Charlotte's sister very poorly tonight. It cannot be long now, and I could tell that the strain is weighing on Charlotte. She was up all last night, all today. All I can wish for them both is peace now, for Charlotte to be able to rest, for her sister to pass quietly. It is cruel to try and hold someone back if the right time has come for them to go.

I wish a peaceful letting go for them both, and for Charlotte, my dear brave Charlotte, the calm that comes from a serenity of spirit, a facing of what has to be, to help her cope with what must come after.

30 OCTOBER

No entry for yesterday. Too distressed to write. Something very disturbing and horrifying has happened, but I MUST face up to it or I will never be able to come to terms with myself, never be able to overcome my problems.

It is now obvious that:

- I AM UTTERLY UNABLE TO HANDLE EMOTIONS.
- I AM AFRAID OF EMOTIONS, AND TO A SHOCKING AND DEBILITATING DEGREE.
- I wrote or said somewhere in these pages that I am an emotional cripple, but that wasn't strong enough. EMOTIONALLY, I DO NOT EXIST.

I am not at all sure after yesterday that I have ever really felt any feelings I could honestly say were genuine for anyone. Were they all part of the act, every good feeling I have ever had, with nothing underneath but emptiness, coldness, a lack of all except a need to protect myself and retaliate against whatever threatens me? Maybe I am deluding myself, never mind anyone else, that I really care or am concerned about others, even the new feelings I have been trying to encourage towards D. and Charlotte.

Sometimes I am conscious of this coldness inside, of scorn and amusement as I watch people interacting among themselves, playing 'games' to get attention and affection. I have been aware of this for years, but it has been so much a part of my innermost self that I have never expressed it. Yet that, I feel, is my secret weapon, my ultimate defence if I should ever be driven that far. The fact that I could turn round at any time and say:

'So you're having a hard time? You're not getting love and understanding, you're lonely, frightened, you have problems? Well, my friend, don't come to me, there's nothing for you here. Offer me whatever you like, *I won't care less.* For me, you don't exist. I have no sympathy, no mercy, no pity. Suffer, weep, die, I shan't feel a thing. I'm not interested, you and your needs just leave me cold.'

From what I have been reading – very cautiously – to try and clarify my situation, it seems this lack of feeling is characteristic of the schizoid personality. The scorn and amusement which makes me feel superior to everyone else, far removed from their futile and childish behaviour, is also symptomatic. I think the reason for it, in my own case, is that I felt so rejected emotionally when I was a child that I in my turn rejected everyone else, and so cannot experience anything for them at all. It is my revenge on those who, in my earliest years, battered me down with 'double binds', ground me into nothing, put me through mental agony, shut me out and left me in the dark.

Okay, you used your big guns on me, and I've learned how much they hurt. What terrible damage they inflict. Now it's my turn. I will reject you – and you – and you – and see how you *like it!*

TO ME, *ALL* EMOTION IS SUSPECT. This is what I discovered yesterday. I was horrified and shocked, but even stronger than my horror was my anger that yet again, someone was threatening me with a big gun. Such terrible fury, such hate, such a desire to avenge the violation I seemed to be experiencing. BUT!!!!??? - what caused all the trouble was not negative, it was something very positive.

Since this is a kind of casebook, I shall type up here the notes I wrote when the incident happened, and describe the actions I took to try and rid myself of the fury and the hate. These have worked up to a point, but I am very drained this morning, and see that I have a long road ahead. Tanya is still fragile and can be knocked out of existence by the power of these old angers, old hates.

It will be a difficult task to try and change myself so drastically, alter my whole attitude to life, to other people. I may if I am honest about what I feel, destroy what I am trying to build. I may drive those who love me away. But if I am not honest, I will get nowhere, and *everything* will be sham, even the new feelings. They have to be shaped and fostered, tested to prove they are genuine. I must go very slowly. The task ahead of me is gigantic. I can only try to work at it bit by bit, a little at a time.

Last night, spent a long time writing (in longhand) the following account of what had happened just previously. It reads as though it all happened in a few minutes, but the writing up took about two hours, thinking, weighing my words to get it accurate. Afterwards I was exhausted from the effort. Am still exhausted, such mental concentration completely drains me.

But had to be done, or I would have lost control of myself and been unable to regain it – perhaps permanently. I *have* to take each obstacle as it comes, and this was the most shattering I have been forced to cope with since I started this diary. Hope I have also taken a step forward by being able to write this account, but suppose I can't know that yet.

*

ACCOUNT OF 'HATE ATTACK'
(written just after it had occurred)

'Tanya has completely gone, whoever is in charge, I don't know. Coped reasonably well with the day, even social contact with a few neighbours, all was well until I phoned Charlotte late in the evening to see how her sister was. Charlotte under great strain, her sister very weak, very restless. The end may come some time tonight. After brief conversation – she does not want to leave her sister for too long – Charlotte closed with what she might have said to a loved daughter: 'Goodnight darling, bless you.'

EDITOR: Charlotte is almost a generation older than Tanya.

'I felt so much love, so much grateful warmth in her voice. She is very low, needs what small strength I can give, was glad I had phoned. But SOMETHING HAPPENED WHEN SHE SAID THOSE FEW WORDS.

'I can only try to describe what the effect was. A cold shock, as though I had been plunged into icy water, rousing every sense to red alert. Danger! Tension in my back, in every muscle. A terrible feeling of blind panic, a numbness inside as though someone had kicked me in the stomach. Followed for a while by uncomprehending bewilderment. I became extremely upset. Hurt, wounded, dazed as the shock wore off.

'I tried to explain how I felt to D. 'As though I'm standing on a rock and I see a great tidal wave sweeping towards me. It's going to flatten me and I'll never be able to get up. Threatened by something. All that emotion, that love – it's going to wipe me out, destroy me. I want to get away, I want to escape from it. It's going to kill me!'

'I wrote earlier in these pages that I could not bear to see *real feelings* in anybody's eyes. I can't handle them. No more now can I handle the overwhelming human love in Charlotte's voice.

'For God's sake, don't love me so much. You don't know what you are doing to me, how panicked I feel, how threatened. YOU ARE HURTING ME!!! I do not want love, I can't take it. And I will run, run to get away from you.'

These feelings passed quite quickly. But in the aftermath of that anger, I have had to get away, be alone. I feel I have been deeply wounded. I want to hit back, to hurt. I feel hate, resentment, and I have got to write it all out or I won't be able to rest.

'Love is a terrible weapon. It left me staggering to be so suddenly struck with it, so assaulted. It's powerful, it hits hard. And I am

155

smarting from the blows. I won't forget or forgive. You DARED to do that to me, to attack me with your love…You bitch, you traitor, you spy…I want to tear you to pieces, I want to wipe you from the face of the earth…

'*NOBODY can do that to me and live. I would strangle you if you were here, I can feel the urge in my fingers, the strength and fury in my heart…YOU HAVE BETRAYED ME…I'll kill you for it. I hate – hate – hate – hate - . And you most of all because you caught me unawares, got inside my defences, turned from a friend to a deadly enemy in those few words. Nearly managed to destroy me…*

'*But I can hit out too. I'm hitting out with all this hate that's burning me up. It can burn you instead, and I'll watch you burn and the louder you scream, the louder I'll laugh…*

'*You're shrivelling to ashes…Your hair's catching fire…You're nearly gone…*

'*And I grind my heel in the embers. I'm free of you. I've killed you, burned you, made you suffer. You're not there any more, you're nothing…AND I'VE WON!!!!!*

*

'Okay, you three, I'm here now. I know you had to do it so that you could get rid of the anger and the hate, so it wouldn't keep me from coming back to you. Let's get out of this place where there's no time into reality. It's twenty past two in the morning, we have to sleep, we have to face tomorrow.

'You've tried very hard Number One, and you *did* do the right thing – not the hating maybe, but the way you got it out of your system. You're a good girl, yes you are, I'm smiling at you, do you see?

'Number Two, you can let the energy level drop now, I want to be able to lie down and rest.

'As for you, Brain, don't start on any of your brilliant ideas – I don't want to know why it happened or what it was all about. Maybe I'll let you think it all out tomorrow – but only *maybe*. We have other things to do as well, and theories aren't the be-all and end-all.

'The main thing is, we've had a nasty attack of hate, but we've managed to get through it without actually letting it hurt Charlotte. She's having a long and difficult night, she's very lonely and very upset – think how *you'd* be in her place. But we haven't hurt her, and we want to be ready to help her tomorrow. If it makes her feel better to love us, we have to learn how to let her - we're learning all the time, getting a bit more used to all these strange new emotions.

'No need to panic. I'm here, and I told you I'd look after you, didn't I? Nobody's going to hurt you. Let's all go to sleep now, try to calm down. It's late, and we're very tired. I'm proud of you, I'm glad you're with me. I need you, but you need me too you know. Come on, it's all over now, and you've earned your rest. Don't worry, little crew, everything's fine, we're all together and we're going to stick together and everything's going to be all right, you'll see. Just try to relax...try to sleep...'

The result of last night's effort and the thinking I allowed the Brain to do this morning: almost total exhaustion, BUT the old bad feelings, the hate and the anger, have been wiped out. There will no doubt be a next time that I have to cope with the same thing, it is not just going to go away, the old patterns will continue to recur – but hopefully I will become quicker and stronger each time.

Have patience, my dear Charlotte, when you read this, please have patience with me. I *want* to learn to love you – and D. - perhaps in time, other people too. I am trying very hard for you, for D., for my daughter. The hate comes, but if I work at it, it will go. There is no anger at this minute, no resentment, none of the bad feeling at all. Please have patience. It will take time, but I am trying as hard as I can.

Evening: News Flashes

Charlotte's sister is very weak, very agitated. Charlotte must return the two hundred miles home tomorrow while another member of the family takes up the vigil. Charlotte very tired, needs to rest. A safe journey, dear Charlotte, a safe journey too for your sister, either through another day or if she leaves you, to whatever place she may be going. For both of you, the knowledge that the end of your journey is where you belong, where it is right for you to be.

Phone call from Joan. She and Vera have been to Barts. The growth *was* malignant but the doctors hope it has not spread beyond the area they have cleared in the eye, though they say 'We can't know'. Vera is unable to have treatment at present, the stitches in her eye are not healing properly. She will be coming back in three weeks.

It is proving a long hard road for these two brave women to travel. I felt I could say nothing that would help, but I can be here at the end of the phone if they want to talk to me. They are trying to face the worst that may happen, and if they can face that, it is the battle won.

31 OCTOBER

The 'hate attack' has proved to be a far bigger thing than I thought, something fundamental, striking at the root of my illness, and hopefully revealing the rottenness that has been hidden for so long. It has taken all my energy, left me thoroughly drained and exhausted, weak, shaky, sick and racked with nausea; it has also been so disturbing that I have had some other very unpleasant reactions.

At first I became terribly depressed, felt hopeless, that there was no point in trying any more. I will not write what is sham, what I do not feel – and yet if I write down honestly what happens, I can see that what I say is shocking.

The viciousness of it, the ingratitude, the cruelty – to turn like that on the person who has stayed with me throughout this journey, been so understanding, so supportive, had such faith in me – to turn on Charlotte, Charlotte, of all people! - and let loose such hate that I wanted to kill her…

I am sunk in guilt. Number One is weeping and wringing her hands. She always knew she was unworthy, she knew she could never do anything right, but this! *This isn't only not right, it's so utterly revolting that Charlotte will never speak to me again, and I would not be able to blame anyone but myself. How could anyone ever want to speak to me again if they were treated like that?*

I am letting Number One cry out her misery for the moment, but I am also bringing in Number Three – the Brain – to shed some light on the situation. *Why,* when Charlotte was in what must have been one of her darkest moments, her sister on the point of dying, herself tired and needing comfort more than ever - why when she expressed her feelings so openly, bared her soul to me as it were, did I choose that instant to plunge in the dagger?

I see it is because, from my own experiences as a child, I came to know the extreme depths of cruelty. I came to know that it hurts more if the victim is at the limit of endurance, if the soul is on its knees crying for mercy.

Oh yes, somebody taught me well! A blow to a healthy person doesn't hurt half so much as if that person is already down, if they have revealed their vulnerability and have given up all pretence. 'I know I can't fight any more so I am asking you, please, you can see how defenceless I am – out of your love, your care, your humanity, don't hurt me. I am as low as I can go, please don't hit me, don't knock me out of existence, won't you give me your hand instead, help me up?

I'm not even trying to fight now, I am asking you, trusting you will hear me, you'll understand, you'll help.'

And *that* was when trust was knocked out of little Tanya Bruce for ever. The hand was never extended, the final thrust always came, chosen with care to do the most damage to what was left of the stricken little soul that had been forced to grovel and beg and plead to be spared the ultimate horror and humiliation and pain. Not only once, but time after time, over years of guilt and shame and misery…

…and what made it worse was that the last blow of all was delivered with the sweetest smile, the loudest 'I love you, Tanya' as the axe crashed home, bit through bone and muscle and sinew and the blood gushed out and I knew I had nothing left of me, nothing at all. I had been destroyed – wiped out – murdered - . And afterwards it was my killer who rescued me, still smiling sweetly, and said, when I could stand up on wobbly legs 'Oh, good, my darling, you're better. NOW WE CAN START ALL OVER AGAIN!!!'

…yes, I know how to hurt, I learned in a good school. And all these forty years, unable to express my anger and my outrage, I have turned them on myself. I have killed myself inwardly, raged at myself, hated myself, put myself through mental torture.

…for, of course, I had to acknowledge that my dear sweet killer loved me with all its heart, always did its best for me, never meant me any harm, was a saint, was perfect, couldn't do anything wrong.

'I sacrifice myself for you, I give you everything I have because I love you so much. I don't ask for any reward, I am too good for that sort of thing but your conscience will tell you, if you are a good girl and listen to it (and I know you are ALWAYS a good girl so far as listening to your conscience is concerned, I have made sure of that) – that you will never be able to repay me for all I have done. You'll always be in my debt, you'll feel terribly guilty, terribly ashamed if you have even the teeniest nasty thought about me – so of course, the fact that I'm going to continue hacking away at you with this axe and it hurts can't possibly be anything you can blame me for, can it?

160

'I give you nothing but good things, so you must be hurting because – well, you know darling, how you have disappointed and wounded me, though I don't complain. After all, it isn't your fault you are such a monster. You can't help it, but I suppose – maybe – the fact that you keep getting hit with an axe and it hurts must be something to do with how awful YOU are - .

What, you're crying? The pain is hurting? But darling, it's nothing to do with me. I have just told you, I only give you GOOD things. I really can't help you, you bring it all on yourself because you are nasty and you think nasty ungrateful thoughts about me. You won't think them any more, will you? It would be so upsetting for me if you did – I honestly don't think I could stand it, you would do me the most frightful harm.'

And the little soul wept: 'No, I understand. I see that it's all my fault, it's nothing to do with you. And I shall never think anything bad about you, or I shall feel even worse than I do with this pain from the axe.'

'That's right, my darling. We understand each other. You KNOW that what I say is true, don't you, because I love you, and if somebody loves you as much as I do, if they sacrifice themselves for you, that PROVES you can trust them, doesn't it? You trust ME. It would be an awful thing if you couldn't trust someone who loves you so much, you KNOW you can trust every word I say because I cannot say a wrong thing, you KNOW that, so however many times I hit you with this axe, you are never going to argue are you, never going to tell me I've got anything to do with it. I would be terribly hurt if you did. I've told you – and you TRUST what I say – that it's all your own fault really.

'I do wish I could help, I really do. I'd do anything for you – see, I'm crying myself – but I do all I can for you, everything a saint can. I pick you up when you're battered and smashed from the axe. I nurse you and bring you back. I always do all I can, and I don't expect gratitude though really, let's face it, you DO owe me such a lot – I'm so good to you that it's unbelievable. But it would only prove you were even more of a monster – and what you ARE is bad enough, heaven knows – if you got angry, if you started to think I was making you suffer, wouldn't it?'

If I am going to help myself, I know I must learn to bring out old angers, old hates. I must learn to express them in some form where I can control them. I learned extremes of cruelty, and in my own defence I too wait for the best moment to strike.

I suppose I cannot know I am doing this. I had no idea I would turn on Charlotte, I was horrified and ashamed, and Number One sank into a morass of guilt. I wrote down the truth, and in the eyes of anyone who is 'normal' the truth will be – as it always was in 'double binds' – just as wrong as a lie. No way can I win. I shall be guilty either way.

It must have been some echo in Charlotte's voice that triggered off suspicion and a desire to retaliate against the love I sensed in her words. I was not writing my hate out at Charlotte personally, but at some faceless 'you' I had to annihilate – at least on paper - to prevent myself from being, in my turn, annihilated.

I don't think it is surprising that to me an expression of love is something to be feared, since in my past experience, what I understood as love accompanied the axe blows and the pain. Love – or what I was told was love – killed me over and over. I suppose I instinctively recoil from it. To me, love is just as threatening as hate. I can't take it; I don't want it; I will violently reject it.

I have to learn with my new self that words *can* mean what they say, that there is no dagger behind the smile, no axe behind the kiss. And I have to learn also to restrain myself from taking my own form of revenge on faceless 'you's from the past who are no longer here. I think this will take a very long time. But the fact that I have been able to bring my anger and my hate into the open, write it out of me without injury to myself or to anyone else, let it go, is I think a tremendous step in the right direction.

Number One has stopped crying now. No need for guilt. We are coping, we are progressing. Even if what is happening is not clear to anyone else, I *know* I have achieved something, that I am moving forward. I have to have faith in myself. I am very sick in mind, and it will take a long time to change my attitudes and instincts and reaction-patterns, but if it can be done, I will do it. We'll get to the end of this road sooner or later, myself and the crew.

The 'hate attack' has not made any difference to my feelings towards Charlotte, though it may take a certain amount of talking to her until I have rid myself completely of any lingering traces of unease. I only hope she can understand what happened, and why.

BUT! Charlotte is not the 'you' who hit me in the past with the axe. I *do* trust her to understand, to put out her hand and not deliver that last blow. I have no right to ask her to do it, I can only trust her, trust that she will help me to believe that there might be a different sort of love. I want to believe there is. I want to learn it so that I can love her back. But it is not easy. In forty years I have only been aware of the axe.

If you will help me, dear Charlotte, I would like to come to believe in the smile instead, without fear, without anger, without hate. I want to be able to learn to smile back at you and know it's a real smile, that *I* don't have to keep my hand on the dagger either.

Much later:

Cannot get rid of depression and guilt. In a 'double bind' about what's happened, of course, the most powerful and destructive of all the 'double binds' I have known.

WHATEVER YOU DO = WRONG = GUILT.

I'm holding onto my lifelines, going back to basics. I *choose* to accept that the truth might upset, might not be clear. But if I was well, I would not need to be writing this diary. I am *ill*, this is my illness talking, my illness feeling so guilty and depressed. It's Number One crying again. I *choose* to accept that it's my illness talking, and believe that when Charlotte reads, she will understand that.

I have done my best to let the old involuntary anger and hate hurt no-one. I have tried to cope with it in a better, more positive way.

Note: There are no such words as 'never' and 'forever'. The Numbers use them because they are still children and they think and feel as children. When they are talking through these pages they are inclined to push all sorts of archaic phrases and expressions from my past into my vocabulary. When I am in control I recognise that these are meaningless.

All things change. What was 'never' yesterday may happen tomorrow. And thankfully, so many things that were 'forever' in the past are starting to slip away.

6
REACHING OUT

2 NOVEMBER

For the past few days I have been trying to deal with the 'hate attack'. Apart from depression, the guilt has been so great that I have been physically ill – nausea, upset stomach, alternating constipation and sudden embarrassing diarrhoea. *Not* a pleasant experience, but I think I have managed to get Number One back into line.

Such terrible guilt has in the past been known to put me right out of action, literally unable to leave the loo for more than a few minutes. Nothing the doctors gave me could cure it, and on the first occasion I went in desperation to a faith healer who said: 'Your feelings of guilt are making you ill – you blame and punish yourself when there is no need.'

Something in those words eased me inside, and I felt absolved so that the physical illness just seemed to pass. It simply went. Now I have to absolve and heal myself, but I am hopeful because in the past I did not know *why* things were happening – now I see I can control them, even though it might drain me utterly in the process.

There was never anything I could do before but suffer and wait for whatever it was to go away on its own – now I can *get rid of it* by dealing with the Numbers. The relief, the sheer relief of knowing where I am going, even if I have not got there yet, is so overwhelming I cannot describe it, a bliss beyond words. I am learning to be 'the master of my fate, the captain of my soul' after a lifetime of fear, helplessness, pain and despair.

It has been a sad weekend for my as yet, small world. Friday brought a late-night phone call from Joan. She and Vera had been to Barts that day and been sent back home for the time being. Though the cancer was removed, the eye is in a mess, stitches not healing properly. Words like 'strangulated', 'they'll dye the eye next time and dig deeper', 'she can't sleep very well because the stitches catch on her eyelid' were not exactly reassuring, but Vera has taken as her watchword that great phrase: TOMORROW IS THE FIRST DAY OF THE REST OF MY LIFE!

In spite of all their courage and determination to face up, though, I fear that there may be many tomorrows of pain and uncertainty for her, dread and fear and helplessness for them both. This morning, I posted them cards to reassure them that if, when Vera comes back in three weeks, she has to stay for treatment, she won't be quite alone. There'll be a voice if she wants to talk, somebody to visit her. Maybe even that small contribution will help, I hope so.

Saturday was a crucial day for Puss. Moira has been finding his need to drink literally pints of water per day – with a resulting flood into his litter tray – rather problematical to deal with, necessitating a lot of cleaning floors where the smell and mess has been carried on his feet. Very worrying. Definitely not normal – can it be his kidneys?

On Saturday he went for tests, the results proved he is sadly an extremely sick cat, in an advanced state of diabetes with renal failure as well. I think I forgot to mention that on a previous visit to the vet, he was diagnosed as probably well over ten years old, difficult to tell as he not only has no bottom teeth, he has no teeth at all.

Toothless, ageing, sick. Not, we think, in pain, but he is too far gone even for insulin injections, nothing to be done, a matter of time only.

Moira brought him home, said determinedly that she'd cope somehow until, as she put it 'he loses his dignity', then it will be more merciful to have him put to sleep. But his last months will, we hope, be secure and as happy as possible. At least he will not die alone, starving and unwanted, a refugee from the bewilderment of losing his former home, his unknown owner who instilled in him such trust and love for the human race. That trust has been justified in Moira a hundred, a thousand times over.

Saturday evening phoned Charlotte's home, since she'd said she would be returning to settle some of the affairs she had to leave so abruptly. She was not there: had set out home but been called back, and her sister had died only an hour before I phoned. Too late for me to make contact, could only send my thoughts and hope they would reach her.

Charlotte's sister had been aware that it was time for her to go, had asked bewilderedly why she was not dead yet, said tearfully that she didn't understand.

'I thought of what you said in The Book', Charlotte told me when she phoned briefly on Sunday - referring to our discussions on suicide, which I have attempted three times, herself once. 'It isn't easy to die.' But her sister is somewhere now where all has been made clear, where there is no more bewilderment but knowledge, certainty and rest in a place where she knew she had to go, where it was right for her to be, where she belongs.

Maybe harder than dying is having to carry on living with the loss of a dear one. Yesterday when I spoke to Charlotte, she was very tired, many threads of ordinary life to pick up, her loss playing itself over and over in her mind.

After the panic and guilt of the 'hate attack' I had a new feeling last night, a deep sadness for all the hurts that my unresolved past hates and angers have brought on others during my life. For me too, I think it has been a letting go, an anguish for things I cannot explain. Why did they have to happen? Why did this have to be? It is not something that tears will ease, no amount of crying or wailing will touch the deep stillness where the sadness lies. There is no blame any more, no anger. Past such trivial considerations. They are surface feelings, they burn themselves out, but in the depths of loss for what might have been, for what never was, for what did exist but exists no more, the whisper will be there always. Why? Why?

To Charlotte in her loss, I can only give my anguish, my sadness, the deep innermost place where that sadness is. Perhaps out of the 'hate attack' came something clean and healing, something that longs to reach out to her and say: I have wondered as well, I do not know either. Please take my sadness, the depth and stillness of it, it is precious to me because I have only just found it, but it is for you if you will accept it. I want to share with you the 'why?' If you will, let us share it together.

I do not know if what I feel is a love free of thorns and daggers. Perhaps love can come as quickly as hate, perhaps it does not have to be learned.

EDITOR:

On the evening of 2 November, Tanya phoned Charlotte and described what had happened during the 'hate attack'. She was distressed because she felt Charlotte would be understandably hurt and offended by its violence and the fact that it had occurred unprovoked, at such a crucial moment. Charlotte's reaction was one of complete understanding, taking a clinical view, offering reassurance that the 'attack' had been positive and valuable in that it had provided information about, and insight into, Tanya's previous difficulties in forming relationships. Since she had not actually been hurt, she emphasised that there was no need for Tanya to feel any guilt.

*

LETTER TO CHARLOTTE
Written by Tanya late evening, 2 November

London

Dear Charlotte,

I'm trying to fight off the guilt, the temptation to crawl and beg forgiveness for wounding you, as no doubt the knowledge of my 'hate attack' will have done however much of a theoretical attitude you take. I'm asking from you more than any human being has a right to ask of another. You're not a psychiatrist who would have been waiting for me to let loose my hate so that he could say 'Good, that was what I've been trying to encourage you to do'. You came into this as a friend, to help me. You didn't ask to get battered and vilified and bashed over the head.

All I can say is, for the first time I'm out on a limb, making a conscious effort to trust in this mess they call the world – trusting you and trusting D., but you most at the moment because it was you who took the full force of the hate. I am terrified. I'm quaking. I am afraid I've come out too far, that as always in the past, the final blow is about to descend, the hand I'm holding is not really there. I've stepped outside my defences, the earth's cracking open, the tidal wave is gathering strength and at the last moment, after reassuring me: Yes, it's all right, I'm here, hold onto me – just as everything crashes on me and I clutch tighter, *then* you will slap my clinging fingers away (the punishment that was always held over for another time) and say: You revolting creature! Don't you *dare* paw me like that!'

And then it's another end for Tanya, but probably worse this time as I've trusted so much more consciously, the disillusion will be so much more unbearable.

I'm holding onto my trust in you as though I'm clinging to a branch hanging over a bottomless precipice, waiting – dreading – terrified - . The branch, is it going to break? Will it crack, shall I fall? If it *does* break, I know that it will be the same old story: Well, you have no-one to blame but yourself! If you hadn't been so wicked and ungrateful to Charlotte, if you hadn't proved you were so thoroughly awful – I always said you'd come to a bad end, and wasn't I right?

It *isn't* always like this, is it? Does it have to be? I only want to know the branch is there, that's all, that the hand won't be snatched away. Please Charlotte, it isn't much to ask, the branch doesn't have to do anything for me, but please, *please* don't break it, don't let me go, not now I've come so far with you, trusted your word, *please*.

Tanya.

PS Please take care of yourself, try to get what rest you can. I'm the last person to be handing out any comfort at all at the moment, more like an extra piling up of the load. Maybe in a while will get back on the straight and narrow – at the moment I'm bloody shaking, this sort of thing is no fun.
God bless.
PSS Hope I might be able to see you soon after Friday – perhaps you'll feel better when the funeral's over, it's an awful ordeal. Loving thoughts, T.
Write when you can – no hurry – also that copy of your poem, the one you're going to read at the funeral. It's a beautiful piece of work. I feel my writing is 'The Cat Sat on the Mat' variety, compared. T.

3 NOVEMBER

This morning I did not exist. Swamped out of myself by something, very shaky, no interest in anything, no desire to communicate. Nothing in the world but misery. It was D.'s care and love that got me to talk. I seem to find it easier to trust a man than a woman – probably because the battles were mostly fought in the past with my mother. A woman is a tyrant, an enemy. I trust D., but my efforts to trust Charlotte are killing me.

EDITOR: Tanya's expectations were obviously not so high so far as men were concerned. She described in the original early chapters of The Book how a man she trusted had raped her at the age of ten, the abuse continuing for nearly two years. She had never been able to speak of these experiences to anyone until she was over thirty.

Managed to say that I felt awful, so racked with guilt. If the other person in a relationship does not punish me, then I have to punish myself. And then – anger came…

Charlotte SHOULD have punished me. Something wrong here. The pattern isn't working out right. If she had punished me, then I could have been angry again, said 'I knew it was no good!' and cut myself off.

Little Tanya ALWAYS has to be punished, the pattern is ALWAYS the same. Tanya is bad, provokes and receives anger, can then be angry herself and that frees her to cut off communications. She is not ALLOWED to do anything and get away with it. Whatever Tanya does is wrong therefore punishment must come from either outside – which lets her hate the other person – or inside – which causes her to hate herself, collapse in guilt and shame, so unworthy she shouldn't be alive among such good, forgiving people - she can then hate them for being good - .

Either way, the pattern works out in Tanya hating, and turning the hate on herself...

'THE PATTERN'S DAFT,' SAID D. THIS MORNING. *What's this?* thought the Brain, perking up a bit. It is true. The pattern *is* daft. There is no sense in it. Everyone has wicked thoughts, but if they handle them and do not translate them into wicked actions, that is triumph – nobody hurt, so why should Tanya feel obliged to do penance?

My God, said the Brain*, if only you'd let me in on this a long while ago, I could have thought it all out for you!*

But of course, that Voice of Authority in the past was for ever thundering: THOU SHALT NOT THINK FOR THYSELF, THOU SHALT HAVE NO BRAIN, ALL THINKING WILL BE DONE FOR THEE! Brain has therefore been in hiding all these years, skulking like a fugitive, never daring to show its face. Only now, after writing The Book, discovering there are three parts of me instead of two frightened children, can I begin to use my brain to work for me.

Thanks to D., thanks to Charlotte, I see the pattern at long last – and the daftness of it. Guilt has gone, I feel better, though still a little shaky. This is a tough road, I could never have travelled it alone. Thank God - or whoever – for my two friends, for their integrity, their patience, their care and love. Somebody up there must have been watching over me to bring me D. and Charlotte.

'No guilt, or I'll be very cross,' said Charlotte, last night.

'You're winning, and you're angry because you know you're winning not losing,' said D.

Thank you, thank you, thank you!

Evening

All tonight a dreadful sense of doom, of melancholy. Just now I started to cry without knowing why. I think Tanya is here somewhere, but I am too tired to try and find her. I feel so lost, terribly alone. I don't know if what I have done, what I have been doing since the day I started The Book, is right. I did not know what I would uncover, the long weary journey, still many miles to travel and I feel I can't do it.

I wondered when I cried what it was that I wanted. Went close to D., held his hand. But there is something else, choking me.

I am wandering in a desolate place, I am weeping inside for my mother. Oh, Mum – Mum – Mum – please come back. Where are you? Don't go away. You were all I had, the anger and the hate and the love all mixed up, and now it's going and I feel so naked, so weak without it. I have nothing to cling to any more. I am so afraid, Mum, I love you so much and I am going away from you. It's breaking my heart, tearing me apart. I don't know if I am crying for you or for me. I am so lost. I need you so much.

What am I going to do? All the landmarks are gone, and Tanya is not able to cope with all the pressures from outside, letters, business affairs. I am afraid she will leave us, and if she does, what will we do?

We can't manage on our own if you're not here and Tanya's not here. We are too little, too frightened. We have lost you and we can't always find Tanya…

I'm here. I'm here. I'm here. Don't cry, little one, I was only resting. I was so tired – I get tired easily you know, I'm only a few weeks old. But I'm never far away.

Dry your eyes, it's all right, I am here. I'm with you. Lean on me. I am strong. I'll help you all, I'll look after you now. You're tired too, you're all very tired, *you* need to rest. These last few days haven't been easy for you – you've worked so hard, done so well, and you are coming through, I'm proud of all of you.

Hold my hands, learn to trust me. I won't fail you, none of you. I'll take the tension and the strain away – see, it's going already – and I'll lift all those worries from you, the fears, the panics. There's no need to worry any more.

Come back from this desolate place, come into the warmth and the light. We'll sit and be peaceful together. I'm with you, I won't leave you. Trust me. Trust me…

4 NOVEMBER

Hard for those terrified little Numbers, but hard for me too. They fight me all the way. When one is comforted, another starts. Number Two keeps trying to struggle for the controls with her manic energy. Number One's guilt is never-ending, no reassurance will stop her misery.

I think it's time to be firm with them. I can't keep on handing out comfort all the time when they are in the same body as me, and I am as tired as them but I have to find the strength from somewhere to cope with their different anxieties, their different panics and depressions and ways of expressing themselves. They do not trust me yet. I am an unknown quantity, a stranger in the camp. But I've *got* to be tougher with them, they are children and they will just keep on and on unless I stop them.

The antics of my personality are continually horrifying me. One bit rushing off screaming *Let me trust, let me love, let me hold you!* Another bit yelling *I don't want to know, keep away, you threaten me!* Someone else trying to shut all the gates, while an equally determined opposite Number is pushing them open.

Come in, come in! on one hand. *Keep out, keep out!* on the other. And all of them driven by the most basic and elemental fear. They never stop being frightened, trying to protect themselves.

This unruly bunch of maniacs, are they really me? Is this what I've been handed to try and work with? - 'Get them into a team, whip them into order, here is your crew, Tanya!' Well, thanks *very* much!

The first priority was to wipe their eyes, stop the chorus of *Help, murder!!!* The next to tell them I was glad to have them with me, that they'd be just fine. *Stop cringing, I'm not going to bite you. You're great! Wonderful! The best! Yes, honestly, I mean it. No, you're not at all inferior, not a chance – whatever gave you that idea? They picked out the best there was for me, I couldn't have done better if I'd chosen you myself.*

BUT! I'm afraid we're going to have to lay down a few ground rules now we're starting to get to know each other. Introduce some discipline and order. No more thinking you're in charge, that it's up to you to sort everything out. I do that, got it? And anyone who tries to argue with me will soon find out who's the boss.

No more big melodramatic scenes, all that weeping and gnashing of teeth. They stop from today, understand? *I mean it!* They're energy-consuming, useless - and boring!

Misery might be all very well for you, Number One, you enjoy wallowing in guilt, but I don't and I won't, so you can cut all that out as from now. Number Two, your methods of trying to solve problems – rushing into 'manias', making instant communication blow the cost or whether it's wise or not – they're just archaic so *they* stop as well. And Brain, all your brilliant thinking is fine but when I want it, please, not any time you decide to indulge in some high-powered know-all-the-answers.

I'm the one who has the problem of trying to make contact with the world out there, and before I can do that I want to know that the world *in here* is in order – no-one deciding to jump up and take the words out of my mouth, spill out apologies for existing. So from now on, you take your orders from me. No use turning your heads away pretending you can't hear me. You hear, and you'll do as I say. Or else!

I haven't been able to make much contact with outside yet, it's a big job. I have to cope with loving, letting out angry feelings, giving and taking, and I can't do any of that if you interfere. So you *stop interfering* and leave me alone. You can do your emotional bits, but dole out the feelings as and when I want them, not plunge us all into misery, guilt or shame whenever you choose to enjoy yourselves.

From now on you listen to me, listen hard. And you obey. ˗

Things are going to be very different for you, I understand that, but they're going to be better, much better, like you've never experienced them before. We've already jumped the first huge hurdle. I know you – and you know me, and we're all in this together. But from now on the old ways are out, the past is scrapped, it's gone. What matters is today, and what we're going to do tomorrow and all the tomorrows after that.

You understand? I have taken over. I am here to stay and what goes is not what anyone else ever said, or what you ever said or did before, but WHAT I SAY. We're going to do it Tanya's way from now on.

7
THE NEW REGIME

Hello, I'm Tanya, and I shall be writing this in future. It's not a diary any more but the story of how a mentally ill writer discovered her three personalities and put them together. And I am writing the end of the story first, here and now, on this page.

I HAVE SUCCEEDED. I HAVE DONE IT. NO MORE A MENTALLY ILL ETERNAL PATIENT, JUST A NORMAL WOMAN WITH THE SAME PROBLEMS AS EVERYONE ELSE. A NORMAL WOMAN. I AM A NORMAL WOMAN.

Of course, I have got to reach the end before I can really write those words and close the covers of this book for good. Today, though, I took my first big step. A revolution, no less. I don't know what put it into my head to turn on those unruly Numbers and lay down the law – the laws, rather, that they've got to obey from now on – but it did the trick.

I am now, at quarter to eleven in the evening, able to report that I have lived my first day as a complete person, as myself. Well, give or take a few minutes struggling here and there. I called the Brain in, for instance, to do some hard thinking, and it didn't want to stop. Give those Numbers a centimetre and they grab fifty metres. But I haven't let up all day, I have fought back when time slipped into the never-never land of standing still, when reality blurred with old past fears and panics as the Numbers tried to force their worry on me.

I have written the end of my story first because I dare not for a second refuse to believe that I might not get there. If I lose faith in myself even for an instant, I'll go under. They are waiting, and as soon as I let go, one of them will pounce. But I'm going to win in the end, even if I have to keep repeating those magic words *a normal woman* to myself on every page.

You'll have gathered, of course, that most of the previous pages were not actually written by me. Some of them were written by Number One, the original 'True Confessions' author and never-ending penitent. Some of them were written at the behest of I-Know-How-To-Do-It Number Two, and some by the greatest Brain of the century – in its own opinion, at least.

But I'm different. I won't give you any sob stuff nor tell you how to do it, nor assure you that I'm the greatest thinker who ever lived. I am an ordinary person. I like myself, I respect myself, I have the dignity I hope to say what I want – within reason – and to feel that it is right for me to have it. I'm a writer. I earn an honest living, and I'm good at my job. I make mistakes like anybody else. I get annoyed, I get angry, I get upset.

I do have a tricky task ahead, but it's something I'd have tackled years ago if I'd realised I was living in this world a bit sooner. I have to start making contact with everyone else. I wrote to my daughter Lara a few days ago, as I am now (though I wasn't so strong an individual then), telling her as simply as I could that I had at forty-three, suddenly and rather unexpectedly discovered that I had never grown up, and was attempting to put the matter right.

I want her to understand, to get to know and love me as I am. It might come as rather a shock – not everybody's mother suddenly changes into a person who wasn't there before, overnight, as it were – but I love her and she is the person I want to reach out to first (except for Charlotte and

D., but of course, they've been here all along, you've met them).

I am so very lucky to have a daughter like Lara, I don't want to lose her. I asked her to write back when she had had time to think about my letter, and I am waiting for her reply with (I admit) a certain amount of anxiety. If she does not understand, if I haven't been able to make contact with her, if she doesn't want to acknowledge me, it will be a sad blow. But if she does – the prospect is thrilling. For the first time ever I shall be a real woman, an ordinary woman with a daughter with whom I can laugh and talk and joke, do all the other things mothers and daughters do when they are together. No more fears, no shadows, though of course there have been happy times in the past.

If I sound slightly breathless, it's because I feel that way. So many things I can do now. I have just realised that there is such happiness in being alive, in loving people, in doing things and sharing things, in being able to take an interest in the hopes of my dear ones, the people I love. When this comes to you at the age of forty-three, it hits you, knocks you over. Life is so precious, so wonderful. I am dazzled, truly dazzled. Every minute is a gift, every experience something to treasure.

When you have been dead and you suddenly wake up and start to live, the joy is boundless. You people who have been living for years, do you realise how lucky you are? What a privilege it is to have people to love, to care about, to share your laughter and your tears? Love is a warm cloak to wrap around you and snuggle into, better than any luxurious furs. And sharing – well, when you've been dead and cold and you've never shared, it's more heady than champagne, more joyous than winning millions.

I could go on like this all night but I have to guard against too much tiredness. Those crafty little Numbers are sitting there with angel faces, good as gold at the moment, but I know that any sign of weakness on my part and they'll be wrestling for control, shrieking about why it isn't right for me to be loving life so much, telling me *they* know better than I do about it all, wanting to sweep me off onto some plateau where I can hold endless discussions with that great Brain that never stops holding forth.

The Numbers can't wait to take over my story again – they think they could tell it so much better than me. But they're not going to get the chance if I have anything to do with it.

This has been a great day. I want tomorrow to be just as good, not spoiled by the fact that I got tired and allowed them to sneak in and grab the controls from me.

Goodnight, lovely world. I'll be back.

COMMENT
by Charlotte

So Tanya quietly takes control of her own self with a small, hesitant gasp of joy, a sense of wonder akin to walking on virgin snow or discovering some lovely secret bay. Perhaps Eliot's *Dust in the air suspended/ Marks the place where the story ended* says it all. For this journey, this story, chose its own end, but the three of us found it at first almost impossible to feel certain of our safe arrival.

None of this exploration followed predictable patterns; certainly I had not anticipated the various events, traumas and emotions to occur as they did; as I said earlier (in The Book), I had no idea what we were in for. The 'descent' and the frenzy of hate – both equally powerful and equally potentially lethal – were, I believe, of enormous importance in enabling Tanya to know and be herself, but had she been a different person, less courageous, less determined, less positive in dealing with her mental problems, she might have been permanently demolished.

Strangely even though it was directed at me (and came at my most vulnerable moment) I knew that the 'hate attack' – perhaps *because* it was directed at me – clarified for her, as it must for anyone who has come this far with us, exactly how negative and how unsound her hates have been and are; so that if one of the crew ever again tries to spring a similar attack Tanya will say, simply and confidently 'Shut up! Look how foolish it was the last time you let rip!' For me, too, it underlined what she had already said about her failure in relating to other people in any meaningful way.

Perhaps this is the right moment to point out how, quite unconsciously, other people and events have been entwined in Tanya's journey: the little cat that was run over, Puss and his new owner Moira, the 'Regent's Park Rowers', Tanya's brother and her daughter Lara, the hurricane, my sister's days and nights of dying, Joan and Vera. Each and all have made some contribution exactly on cue; so much interweaving. Our lives over the last weeks have truly emphasised Donne's *No man is an island.*

After reaching the end of the diary, Tanya told me of the lovely card she had received from Vera and Joan. In it they had written 'Thank you because you are you'. If they had searched for weeks they could not have chosen any better words to say at that particular moment because, as she and D. and I emphatically agreed, that is precisely what it has all been about – enabling Tanya to be the person she really is: someone who is kind and generous, affectionate and tender, joyful and intuitive with a good brain (notice I do not use a capital B!) and a lively sense of humour for good measure. In other words, a normal woman with the frustrations, fears and fervours we all have.

It would be very foolish to draw any heavyweight conclusions, make any comparisons. There is no need. Tanya has reached an understanding of herself in a way and at an age that many people never achieve. She has accomplished her own wholeness. Like the rest of us she will have setbacks and doubts, but I have total faith that, come what may, she will stay true to herself.

182

PART TWO

1
SEVEN WEEKS LATER

Some seven weeks after the last entry in her diary, Tanya once again felt she needed Charlotte's help. From their discussions:

Charlotte: I gather it's been a bit tougher than you expected, Tanya.

Tanya: Well, I came to the end of the diary – or at least, I felt in myself that it had ended and there didn't seem to be any need to write any more – I assumed that was it, I had gone as far as I could go. As you wrote, we were surprised, but we just seemed to have naturally 'got there'.

I suppose the ultimate aim of the journey I made – we made – for myself and possibly for you, or for anyone else who does something similar or wants to follow it through by reading about it, is a deeper understanding that will make it easier to cope. What I have found, though, is that the understanding I might have achieved by going through the whole experience – the journey – writing The Book and then the diary – seems to have made things more difficult rather than easier.

I can understand now why it's so frightening to do this sort of exploration of yourself – why so many people fight it – because in a way, the understanding seems to be more of a burden than a release. Maybe sometimes it's easier not to know, ignorance can be bliss. In my case, the knowledge I have achieved about myself has ruled out many things that seemed to hold out hope of some sort before I started to understand myself. Now I know these are dead ends.

Charlotte: Probably by ruling out so many things, you also increased your expectations that having reached this degree of understanding of yourself, you would be more able to stay in charge. But I think you *have* stayed in charge.

Tanya: Yes, maybe you see the difference in me more than I do myself, but I'm not really sure whether I have been in charge, you know. When I 'took over' the Numbers and felt myself to be in control – which I did – it was marvellous. I hadn't actually intended to finish the diary there, but for days afterwards I found myself thinking there was just no more to say, so that was why I stopped writing.

Tanya was very much there, the Numbers were more or less in order, there was a clear way to go. But I have found in the weeks since that unless one lives in a vacuum or on a desert island where you're the only inhabitant, one has to stay in that very deep layer of thought all the time, thinking through every minute of every day, considering every action, every reaction, pressure, stress - .

Charlotte: Which would be impossible.

Tanya: Yes, quite impossible, and there have certainly been occasions where I have known I was not in charge. Well – I was aware that I wasn't, put it like that. In a way I suppose I was much better than at the time I was writing The Book and the diary, because at least I didn't feel the need to rush off on my own to write it all down and order Number Two back into her seat or something.

It has been as though, over all, I was in charge but I knew something was not right – and I haven't always been able to put it right. Every small thing would have involved a detailed exploration through several days in order to determine which 'double bind' I was in and what was causing it – all the things I did at the beginning of the diary each time there was an upset, you know? But I can't do this all the time – one would have to work awfully hard at it and do nothing else but keep analysing thoughts and feelings every minute of the day. It would be terribly limiting and I don't want to spend all my life doing that.

So I have been getting on with other work, trying to pick up everything I dropped to do The Book and the diary, trying to live more or less normally. But I feel there is more to say, that the journey is by no means over. In fact, the further on we seem to get, and the more we seem to have got to 'the end of the story' – and as you know, we've already passed that stage several times, I've said to you 'That's it, I think the worst is over now' – well, the more we seem to get to the end, the more I seem to see 'the end' as, not so difficult to get at, possibly, but further away even than it seemed at the beginning. Does that make sense?

It's as though what I have done have been short term things, but in the long term, I don't know whether there is any end at all for me. I don't see how there can be.

Charlotte: Don't think I'm belittling what you have achieved, but surely nobody's journey for understanding of themselves, for trying to cope with their problems and difficulties, is actually ever over until their physical end.

Tanya: No, I don't think it is, but this realisation, coming to see now that whatever I might decide to do as myself, as Tanya, I will never reach a point where there is any end at all to my struggling until I am dead – that's a terrifically frightening thing to have to face. I suppose it's obvious really, but somehow it had never dawned on me before, and then it just seemed to hit me – it doesn't matter how hard I try, how much I want to get myself in perfect order, there will never be any end, I'll never really be in control of myself until I am dead – well, that is a horrible thought.

To realise that the struggling and conflict is never going to stop – well, it makes me wonder why I started all this in the first place. I thought it would make matters easier – it hasn't made them easier. They've possibly become clearer but the struggle and the conflict is still very much there. I've seen the pattern more since I finished the diary, because obviously I didn't stop thinking things out, even though it wasn't on such a very deep level. In my case there is great conflict between wanting to relate to other people and wanting to be entirely free from them on my own. The love/hate syndrome we've talked about before.

I don't think this can ever be cured. I don't think there is a cure for it, as such. It's something that was done, something happened to cause the split in me, and it cannot be undone.

I hoped, as I put in The Book and the diary, that I might be able to learn to trust, but I'm having to face the possibility that it is something I will never be able to do. I am coming to see that it is a bad flaw in me that I can never cure.

Charlotte: No, I don't think you'll ever be able to actually 'cure' yourself, but the fact that you recognise this as a difficulty, this inability to trust - .

Tanya: By the way, it doesn't apply to you.

Charlotte: Ah, but it does apply to me, it did apply very much to me with the 'hate attack'. You're turning your back on the truth here, not wanting to admit it.

Tanya: Well – maybe, but I do want to say that you are the only person I would trust enough to speak about all this with, even now, as far as I've gone. You are the only one I'd get in touch with, say 'Look, Charlotte, there's some more I'd like to discuss, will you talk to me about it?' I wouldn't go to a psychiatrist, to anybody else with the confidence and the trust, however limited, that I have in you.

Charlotte: But is there still some part of you – be honest – that's waiting for me to turn round and do you down?

Tanya: I'm afraid there is, probably.

Charlotte: In which case, it most definitely does apply to me. But it's still possible for you and I to have a friendly, working relationship. So what I'm trying to say is, the fact that you're probably never going to be able to change means: **a.** You've got to learn to accept yourself as you are, and **b.** That doesn't mean relationships are out for you.

We both know from the co-operating we've been doing that you do have a fundamental difficulty, to which I was at risk the same as everybody else, because you did have that 'hate attack' at me and you've just admitted (rightly, I think), that you're basically deep down waiting for me to turn on you with some hurt still. But we've managed to stay friends, so I don't think you need despair at having to go through life with this flaw, as you put it.

Tanya: I think a great deal of the credit for us being able to stay friends – and probably better friends than we were before, I hope so anyway – more understanding and useful to each other, or whatever friends are supposed to be – well, Charlotte, in my opinion most of the credit is on your side, not mine. I do my best and you've been understanding of my disabilities, flaws, whatever you call them, but since writing The Book and the diary, I've had to try and make contact again with everybody else – family and so on – as though I was a new person. I've done it very hesitantly, without going into details, but I've found that no-one else – not one person – has been able to accept me as you do, so I can be myself, my new self, with them. It's like trying to communicate through gauze. I might not have seemed different to them, but *I* have known I was different, and I've found that the relationships which existed previously were no relationships at all from my point of view. But I couldn't seem to establish any new ones because everybody else simply carried on in the same old way and wouldn't – or couldn't – see what I was trying to do.

In a peculiar kind of way, I think everybody would be quite disturbed if I announced that I was actually very much better and far more in control. They seem to *prefer* me to be the way I have always been, doing the things they can shake their heads about, and getting depressions that land me in mental hospitals. They are familiar with that, and they'd rather have it because that's the Tanya they know, than have to try and come to terms with a new, better relationship with a more normal Tanya who can say: 'Yes, I'm all right really, it's just that I have a few flaws.'

Charlotte: I think you have to accept that if other people have not yet reached the point where they are able to understand, they are bound not to respond to any other relationship than the one they know. Even if you tried to explain, you'd probably meet with an almost aggressive misunderstanding or else total disinterest. But Tanya, that is a failure of *their* comprehension – other people's disabilities, if you like – rather than a disability or failure of yours.

Tanya continues

My self-knowledge, such as it is so far, seems to have brought a terrible feeling of isolation with it, and increasing frustration that once again I seem to battering vainly on doors or gates that are shut to me. The depression, the psychosomatic illness, the conflict within, has been increasing in intensity, all but crippling me from trying to live in any normal manner again. It is ever-present, waiting when I wake, preventing me from sleeping. I know that the children in me, the Numbers, are fighting desperately for their survival. I told Charlotte I seem to be experiencing a most grievous sense of sadness and loss, as though I am mourning deeply.

'Will I never be able to find peace?' I asked her despairingly. She said: 'What peace, exactly?'

As always after talking out my feelings to her, I began to see everything in a better perspective. Things I have read, even things I have written myself, come back to me, and with them meaning and significance. I always imagine that each set of struggles will have to be resolved before I can proceed, and do not realise that often, I am actually fighting in the wrong war. Once I try to pin down what the battle is all about, the same thing happens as at the end of The Book: the enemy, when identified, becomes as insubstantial as mist. The struggle is miraculously eased as the pain lifts of its own accord.

I told my daughter when I wrote to her that I have been going through the process of 'growing up'. But I have un-knowingly been shutting my mind to what 'growing up' is all about. Within myself as within us all, are the 'children' I have come to know, the Numbers, as well as the newly-discovered 'adult' part of me. I thought it would be enough simply to be aware of these entities, but it is not. As an 'adult' I have to relinquish the longing for guidance and for some outside adult to 'take care of me', tell me what to do, organise my life.

I said in The Book that I had only existed through others. This has been true for all my years of living because I was trapped in 'double binds', unable to take any action on my own initiative. Everything I did depended on whichever Voice of Authority had decided (or been forced) to assume responsibility for me, and the only way I could break free of the orders I was given (or even the lack of orders) was to indulge the manic 'child' in the tantrums which were the only means by which I could express my own self.

Now I am learning to curb that wilful child whose wishes and actions are as irresponsible as wanting to rush into the road when traffic may be passing. But simply curbing the 'manias' is not enough. I have to learn to let my own adult personality make my decisions, plan my course, think for me, and not cling to my child-like dependence on others. It sounds so much better, of course, to be 'master of my fate, captain of my soul' but what I had not realised before was that I would find it well-nigh impossible to let the 'children' inside me go for ever.

With adulthood one gains freedom but one also has to accept responsibility for oneself: one has to face the fact that *one cannot blame others.* Everything I do in the future, whether it is wise or foolish, will be because I myself chose to do it, not because 'it was the right course of action, Tanya', or because 'you know right from wrong', or 'it will please somebody else', or even because 'I need you to do it' or 'this is what I'm telling you to do.'

The prospect of taking complete responsibility for my self, something I have never been able to do, is to me horrific and terrifying. I am shaking inside at the very thought. No more will I be able to turn to someone else for comfort, lay down the burden of my fears and worries and find the peace that comes when, knowing more capable hands will solve all my problems, I can forget about them and sleep like a child in the consciousness that someone more 'grown up' will deal with everything for me.

No more can I say defensively that I didn't have any choice, it was something I got pushed into, I can't help it if it went wrong. Because now I know there *is* a choice, that it is mine to make, and if something does go wrong the responsibility is mine alone and I must accept it - accept too my failings, my mistakes, my inability to be perfect, the fact that sometimes I will hurt or upset others, and that whatever happens I can no longer run to hide my face in someone else's shoulder and shut my eyes or even say: 'I don't feel well enough to cope. You do it for me.'

In the past I have always, in the end, run away when life became too difficult. It brought me no peace and it buried me beneath an unbearable load of guilt and shame. I must begin to turn and face up. I must make my own choices, take on my responsibilities, find strength within myself and not wait for some voice to tell me what to do, or somebody to say: 'I need you, Tanya.' I have to try and discover my own wisdom, and have the courage to abide by it.

There were further revelations from my subconscious as in The Book, which helped to clarify the situation for me at this point. I made notes but my mind (the Brain) was working so quickly that I could not type them up and elaborate on them before I had reached what seemed to me to be the real root of the problem. Since they illustrate how my awareness developed, I give them as they are:

'I don't mean that the child in me must go for good – the child's qualities are necessary and valuable. But I must let the child relinquish trying to cope, and trust myself as an adult – trust Tanya, the real adult me.

'My adult is never sure of itself – it shies away when confronted by other adults. I seem to be able to relate easily to other grown-up people who are 'children' to whom life is a game. With true adults, especially when they are appreciative or critical, the child defences in me take over.

'I have been blaming others for not understanding, in other words I have been doing just what I told myself my adult must not do. I have been PUTTING THE BLAME ON OTHER PEOPLE – 'it's their fault' - transference? Is the blame really MINE?

'The adult has been fighting all the time in me for recognition, but terrified when recognised. I feel my adult is powerful, but unacceptable – capable of destroying others (perhaps I felt it would destroy my mother if revealed, since she was largely a frightened child herself). I will not use it, this weapon. My own self is too powerful, must not be allowed expression – I haven't learned to handle the power - .

'There is cruelty there. I get into a position where I can strike to kill, as I did with Charlotte, at the best possible moment. I worm my way into people's hearts to discover their weak points, I know just what will hurt most. I could destroy them, I know what to say to get right at their inmost being – '

(When I was reading out these notes to Charlotte and she asked: 'Do you ever say these cruel things?' I was horrified.

191

'No, never, never. I would bend over backwards not to hurt anyone, I try not to argue or have rows, I always feel that if something terrible is said it can never be rubbed out, never forgotten, never retracted. I would never say hurtful things, but I know the weapon is there and if I wanted to, I *could* say them, I could destroy others.')

I wrote in The Book that after all 'manias', particularly those that have involved men, I have wanted to wipe them out completely. I wrote that if my conscience (or something) had not restrained me, I might have been a psychopathic killer. Even then, when I was completely unaware of any of the self-knowledge I have gained during the writing of The Book and the diary, at the very start of my journey into myself, I knew the truth without realising it.

The last few sentences of my notes brought me face to face with it again, and with what I hope I have now recognised as the real enemy. It is myself.

'PERHAPS I WON'T TRUST OTHERS BECAUSE I KNOW THAT DEEP DOWN, NOBODY CAN TRUST ME. I WILL TURN AND STRIKE AT THEM – I KNOW I AM CAPABLE OF THIS.'

The thinking through of my notes has taken over a week, but I have come to see that the whole crux of the matter is TRUST, not only of other people but of myself.

I do not trust others, I cannot trust others because I do not and cannot trust myself. I do not know what trust is, I have no understanding of it. And the lack in relationships is not on the part of others, but my own lack. My feelings of isolation are of my own making. Since I lost the ability to trust, and put up defences to enable me to know where to strike if I was threatened, I must have been unable to relate to anybody at all in any meaningful way.

No wonder so much of my life has seemed as though I was acting a part, that I have never felt I could be 'just me'.

What little self I had was shattered, and the pieces (the Numbers, I suppose), have been on a continual alert ever since, never weakening their vigilance for a single second. I realised today that I have no expectation at all of kindness, consideration, affection. If any of these are proffered I am either so deeply touched that I feel I can never repay such bounty (one unexpected kind word from a stranger can have this effect), or else I react with intense suspicion.

Anything given to me is suspect. I want to know the motive. I want to know where the poison is hidden in the casket, where the adder lies curled, what is the real meaning behind those words 'I love you, Tanya.'

I can take nothing from anybody, no gifts, no love, no kindness, no warmth. Mentally, I refuse to place myself under the obligation to repay the debt (which I am emotionally unable to do). I will not accept love because since I trust nothing and no-one - as I must have revealed to everyone else as well as myself when I had the 'hate attack' at Charlotte - love is just as threatening to me as deadly enmity. I will allow no-one past my defences, and if they come it is at their own risk, for I can see now that I might at any moment turn and stick my own dagger mentally into their throat.

I can switch off feelings of love (not consciously, it is done without my own volition) at the snap of a finger, and what is left is complete indifference. The heart is icy cold, my emotions are something separate, something I haven't yet been able to sort out at all – the monstrous and monumental revelations I have just been detailing are enough to try and cope with at the moment.

I have got past being horrified and ashamed at what I find within myself, there has been so much to be horrified and ashamed of on this journey. And if I am as I am, I don't think the blame is mine, but I cannot blame anyone else for it either, since the 'double binds' that put me here and destroyed my trust were merely the expression of other people's own inner torments. It is spilt milk, no use crying over.

Okay, so this is what I have to accept as the person I am. I am tracking her down slowly through these pages – and hopefully, trying to face her honestly rather than squirming out and saying, 'Oh no, that's not me, I could never be like that, there must be some mistake.'

Every time I feel the need to confer with Charlotte, I am coming to see that it means I have reached a point where there is something I am refusing to face because it is too painful. Charlotte does not tell me the answer – she cannot know it – but somehow, she gives me the courage to look the nasty fact straight in the eye and acknowledge it. And though at the moment I may not be able to understand her trust and faith in me (as well as that of D.), I thank God, or whoever, that though both of them are within my gates and liable to have mental daggers stuck through them if I feel too threatened, they are still with me, still caring and keeping the lines of communication open.

From my reading up on psychiatry, I think I have just described a schizoid personality which got that way through being subjected to 'double binds' in childhood. This seems to be the only thing that fits my own honest assessment of myself (as honest as I can be, until I discover more), so I suppose I have found out now what my 'label' is, what I am and suffer from. But that's not the end, folks, not for Tanya. A 'label' isn't the answer, the thing is, what do I do about it? Is there any cure? My guess is that in this case no, there isn't.

If I can't take it away, I have to learn to adjust, to accept it and try to work out some way of living normally – as normally as I am able, since I see no point in trying to kid myself that I am ever going to be able to have the kind of relationships that people who do not have my difficulties are able to have. I must come to terms with the fact that certain things WILL be difficult for me, so in order to avoid unhappiness and misery for myself as well as others (since my own state will obviously affect people close to me) I must not try to do what I can't do.

I must make the most of what I *can* do, and do it as well as I am able. In fact I feel the urge to write at this point, in what I hope is a positive manner: This is where the story *really* starts...

2
THE LEGACY OF CHRISTMAS

Several days since I almost persuaded myself my problem was just a trivial little thing I could come to terms with. I have spent Christmas with Lara and Neil, my daughter and son-in-law, I have had more thoughts and begin to see that this whole question of trust goes far deeper than I imagined. I am not sure if I will be able to do anything about it. I am not even sure whether I want to.

Over Christmas, Lara and Neil were warmly welcoming and loving, and touched me to the heart with their thoughtfulness, their consideration in ensuring I had a restful and enjoyable time. No sloppy sentiment – Lara is not like that – but carefully chosen little gifts, an acceptance of my foibles, no comments on my slightly odd behaviour. Yet during the whole time I was with them I was hardly able to sleep, and collapsed with exhaustion when I got home. I had shared the long hours of Christmas night with a black sky in which there was one small star, and their soft-furred and contented white kitten.

When they said goodbye, Lara hugged me. 'It's been lovely to have you, Mum, lovely to see you.'

I mentioned this to an old friend (who is not aware of the therapy I am subjecting myself to) and said rather wryly: 'I hope it wasn't too bad for them, my being there.'

'Of course it wasn't,' she replied briskly. 'That is a fault of yours, you know, being unable to accept things gracefully. It spoils people's pleasure in giving to you.'

My first question: Why couldn't I sleep? Why am I never able to sleep when away from home – and sometimes not even here? Why, when I am burning-eyed and helpless with exhaustion, can I not relax and get the rest I crave?

I have deduced that it is because I have all my defences on the alert in case I need to protect myself. But why against D.? Why against my daughter and Neil, who would never dream of harming me? It goes deeper than not trusting. D. said: 'It's as though you were apprehensive all the time.'

My second question: Why was I convinced in spite of Lara's hug and kiss, her reassurance they had been glad to have me, that as soon as I had gone they would say to each other: Thank God for that! Am I (I begin to wonder) getting paranoid? I don't know the answer. One 'label' is enough for now – I may not even have that one right.

But looking back, I can see that this is not some recent problem. I have always had trouble sleeping, going right back to childhood, and I have always had the feeling that as soon as I walk out of a room everyone else will heave a sigh of relief. I have always been, as I described in The Book, mentally prepared to pack up and move on since I have never felt I was wanted, wherever I was. And though on one level I can be touched by my daughter's thoughtfulness and love, on another I do not really believe even Lara when she says, 'It's been lovely to have you, Mum.'

Not only do I not trust, not only am I basically unable to accept anything from others, not only do I not believe what everyone else ever says to me and think I must be wary because they have that dagger hidden behind the smile, I can see that I BELIEVE, IN MY HEART, THAT EVERY PERSON I EVER MEET, EVERYONE WITH WHOM I COME INTO CONTACT, IS ACTING A PART.

I have had to act a part all my life. I therefore believe that everyone else is doing the same. They smile - but if they decided to drop the mask, they could switch off that smile.

197

They love me – but if they found it did not suit them they would just turn it off. I must be ready for when the mask drops, when I see what is really behind the warm kiss and the loving hug.

I see now that I am even more isolated than I thought. I have mentioned that I have no expectation of care or affection, kindness or warmth. I do not even have that expectation from D. But my greatest 'double bind' is that if the warmth and kindness is there, I cannot take it. I cannot trust it because I believe it to be a cover for something far more sinister. One simply does not get given anything for nothing. One does not even get loved for nothing. One has to pay. And I suppose I must have decided long ago that the cost in suffering and pain was too high.

I do not really think I have ever loved anybody. I have needed them, wanted them, been torn with pity, compassion, tenderness, a desire to help, to give – but love? What is that? Looking back, to me it is a 'mania' that burned itself out and left me wanting nothing but to get away and destroy the evidence. Or a hearts and flowers throbbing of emotive violins; a delusion that would vanish with the dawn; a pink card with bows - 'A Little Girl – now your life is complete!' All so persuasive. So throat-catching.

I would like to be able to love my daughter, and yet even her warm hug and kiss cannot persuade me – not *really*, in my inmost soul – that she and Neil would have said to each other when I had gone, 'It was so nice to have Mum with us.' Even a tape recording of those very words, I would suspect had been made purely out of kindness, because they wanted me to feel better rather than spontaneously.

Nearly every conventional word of love I say (maybe every one) is part of the act I have performed all these years so people will not suspect the awful truth – that there is nothing inside me for them. I have given everything away – handed myself out in chunks, given time, energy, understanding, my talent, my thought processes, reassurance, help, care. But beneath *my* mask there have been only my defences waiting, and the desire to persuade others that *they* were not unloved, unwanted, uncared for. If that is a contradiction, I cannot explain it. Maybe someone else could, but I only know how I feel.

This must be why I have been suffering a sort of mourning. Maybe I could see it coming in my sub-conscious – because when you get down to it, I am having to face up to the fact that WHATEVER I THOUGHT I HAD, OR WAS, I am having to let it go. It is sad indeed when you discover you are afraid to trust the world – even the love of your own daughter – because you will accept and acknowledge no emotion at all, either from her or within yourself.

More than a day with anyone and I know from experience – and from being realistic with myself – that I become restless, begin to count the hours so that I can get away and feel free, remove the imposition my presence is forcing on them. Even with D., I wait without realising it for the evidence that I have to pay for the care and love he gives me. And though he is possibly unaware of it, that evidence always comes, making me frustrated, angry, irritable. I long to be free from the burden of his affection, to be alone.

I was wrong to say that I can destroy others. That has been how I have felt, but it is merely a symptom.

'Aha!' said the Brain. 'That is left over from childhood. A very crafty psychological mechanism, my dear Tanya. You *think* your anger and hate would destroy others, but you wouldn't really be able to destroy them at all.'

And it is true. These awful weapons I have been storing up, they have shrunk to popguns. I might say a few sharp words, but much to my amazement the victims wouldn't expire, they would probably just come back with a few home truths themselves. And possibly *that* is why I am afraid to use my anger and hate.

I am beginning to see that in mental illness, or personality disorder, or whatever it is that I have, everything is turned round like Alice-Through-The-Looking-Glass. WHAT I FEAR IN OTHERS IS REALLY SOMETHING I AM AFRAID OF IN MYSELF. I blame them, but it is me who is at fault.

Since quite a lot of this sort of illness is rooted in the early years of living, I feel that perhaps many mentally ill people are still suffering as I did – and possibly still am – from the child in their personality running riot. It is my Numbers which cause all the trouble – though whether I can blame them for the great Lack of Trust, I don't know. Perhaps I would be able to feel differently if I was completely the adult Tanya all the time. Perhaps if I could stop acting myself, I wouldn't think other people were acting. Perhaps if I could be completely honest, I would believe others. If I could trust myself not to turn on other people, possibly I could relax a bit, begin to trust them not to turn on me.

At this point I had several revelations of thought in quick succession. I am sure that I have been finding and then losing the answers to all my problem throughout this diary, so I am going to write them in big letters here so I don't forget them again.

I CAN CHOOSE TO ACCEPT THE WORLD AS IT IS, MYSELF AS I AM.

The last words in The Book, and yet I still don't see that this is what I must do.

ACCEPT MYSELF.

First of all, accept myself. As I am. I thought I had done this, but I have not. If I accept myself I must take all the parts of me, not just the 'good' bits. I think Tanya will accept the Numbers, but THE NUMBERS WILL NOT ACCEPT

EACH OTHER. And maybe this is what has been wrong all the time. When you accept someone, you do not stand in judgement on them – and my God, how I stand in judgement on myself.

I have to learn to accept myself, to like myself. Then maybe I can believe that if I can like myself, other people aren't kidding when they say they find Tanya Bruce quite likeable too. But straight away, something inside me shrieked:

*You? How can **you** possibly like yourself? Just look at all these awful things you've been telling us – you have NO FEELINGS! People hand things out to you yet you actually admit you DON'T TRUST THEM, you DON'T BELIEVE THEM, you WANT TO GET AWAY FROM THEM! What would Lara say if she knew that all her love and care at Christmas hadn't even touched your miserable flinty heart? It's no wonder you don't like yourself, that people don't like **you**! You are IMPOSSIBLE TO LIKE! You are unworthy, vain, sham, just something that crawled from under a stone. The sooner the better you go back there, and stop giving me hysterics by suggesting you might be LIKEABLE!*

I recognised that voice, mercifully. It's Number One, the eternal penitent, quoting a Voice of Authority from the past and beating her breast in horror as the enormity of her sins slams home. I'm a little nearer to the truth now. Maybe the other Numbers accept each other, but NUMBER ONE DOES NOT ACCEPT HERSELF! I cannot take myself as I am because she will not let me. She feels her guilt at the mere fact of her existence so violently that it spills over all the other parts of my personality.

To myself, I am unloveable, unlikeable. Not just got a bit of an inferiority complex, but can never apologise enough to the rest of the world for taking up space, for using the air I breathe. It is Number One who is always saying 'I feel awful about this' or 'I hate myself but - ' or those words I must have said more times than any others in my life: 'I'm sorry.' I am always sorry. Sorry to be a nuisance, sorry to be in the way, sorry to impose, sorry to bother you, sorry to have to ask, sorry to disturb you, sorry, sorry, sorry.

Well, the faithful Brain has come up with this question for Number One: IS IT ANY BETTER YOUR WAY? Wanting to please others, making sure they don't feel unloved, uncared for, unwanted – isn't this whole thing just one big con trick? You want others to feel loved - so you *pretend* you feel something, just go through the motions and say the right things. But do you imagine other people are so dumb they don't know the difference between the real thing and your act, however saintly and good you think you are being? Who are you kidding?

Number One, you are *worse* than I am. At least I'm trying to be honest. I'm trying to be straight, and I can be proud of myself for that. But what have you got to be proud of, or likeable for? Your whole world is just one enormous lie, everything you say is fake.

How can I accept pathetic little Number One? I have read that people who have suffered from 'double binds' will treat their children (and others) in the same way, so that it can go on and on down generations. And Number One has in fact doled out exactly the same treatment to others, that I felt hurt me so much when I was on the receiving end. So how can I like that part of me?

How can I accept the knowledge that I may have hurt Lara through my inability to accept her love? That I hurt others by 'refusing to take gracefully' and spoiling their pleasure in giving to me? If I can see through the smile to the dagger behind it, others can see through my smile, see the dagger I hold at the ready as well.

I want to break this for good and all. I have to struggle free of the most basic 'double bind' there is, that I MUST accept and like myself, and that I feel I CAN NOT accept and like what I am. I know in my bones that only this way will there be peace for me. Only this way will I (I hope) be able to reach Lara and Neil and D. and Charlotte.

Charlotte's voice at the other end of the phone, always there, always warm and giving even after the 'hate attack'; D.'s trust shining out even in my most prickly and impatient moods; Lara and Neil's carefully wrapped pile of little gifts that surely no other Mum of forty-three got last Christmas (a badge that said 'I am 21', for instance, a little bar of soap printed with 'I Love My Mum'), their kisses at the station as we parted for what will probably be many months until I see them again – the thought of all of these is making me cry. Other things too. Vera and Joan sent me a beautifully illustrated volume of prayers and readings with the title *More Precious than Gold*, and Joan said: 'That's what you are to us, we knew it was for you as soon as we saw it'.

I cannot let them all down. If they see something in me that they love, I must believe in it and find it too, so that I can love myself.

3
HELLO AND GOODBYE

Hello, it's me again, Tanya herself, in person.

They nearly got me that time. I was certain I was off the rails because after having a good cry as I wrote those last pages, I had landed myself in what was obviously an Impossible Situation. What can I do, I wailed at D., I can't see how I can cope with this. Should have realised what my loving little Numbers were doing then, except that I was so very tired – making me unable to sleep is one of their weapons, they have quite a refined line in mental torture considering that their emotional age is probably zero! But now I have managed three hours sleep, and I'm writing this before things get any more out of hand.

There is only one problem – a 'double bind'. And only one answer – Tanya must *break it* or she will go under.

Breaking it is exactly what I'm doing at this moment. They tried to put me off – ' – but I feel too dozey, can I really be sure? – oh, I do feel sick, it would be better to rest, and this is such a big one to tackle – (sob sob, weep weep)'.

But I am determined as you see, and – as I knew it would – the sickness, the misery, the guilt, the tired feeling, the tension, is all fading as I do what I have been trying to do all along. **HOLD**. Hold myself. Hold onto the fact that I have accepted myself. Yes, I did, if you recall, in the last entry in the diary before I stopped writing it, when I thought the battles were all over. And when I am fully myself, in control, I may still be a bit shaky on confidence but I do have enough sense of being to avoid the traps laid for me by those cunning little Numbers – Instant Guilt! Turn-On Sentimentality disguised as 'Deep Feeling' – Eternal Doubt! (Do not trust yourself because you have even worse problems you aren't even aware of yet! Etc).

I have only one main problem. Getting trapped in 'double binds'. And I have only two enemies who are out for my death. Number One and Number Two (I think the Brain is on my side), working in perfect harmony. AND THAT'S IT! Anything else I can cope with.

Difficulties in relationships? I'll get over them somehow, given a little time to work things out. Emotions? No problem. *I* can love, *I* can trust. If not, I would not even be writing this, or discussing the pages as I do them with D, or turning to my dear, dear friend Charlotte when I feel down.

I most certainly will need help in the future – I don't kid myself that this pattern isn't going to happen again and again. But so long as I can keep out of 'double binds' and hold onto myself, I'll survive – and so will everyone else within my orbit. *I* can get along fine with them, but unfortunately, I do have that little crowd of imbeciles I have to take everywhere with me, who always do their level best to throw a spanner in the works and foul things up. Skeletons in the cupboard, death's heads at the feast – they've got nothing on my Numbers, and if I can keep them down, I reckon I am doing the whole of humanity a service, as well as myself.

I had seen the problem coming, I was aware of it to some extent, yet it still got me. It was, of course, Christmas, which is the most stupendous 'double bind' ever invented. Next year I shall be more wary and try to approach it differently. I shan't say: Oh dear, the crowds! the commercialism! having to make journeys by bus and train, standing all the way in the cold and arriving with Siberian feet! being obliged to buy and send cards, stand in Post Office queues for hours, try to think what gifts people will want, wonder whether the postal strike will be on or off! the shutting down of all my business contacts for the party season! the frustration! the hell of a modern-day Christmas of computers and affluence!

No, next year I shan't pretend it doesn't exist. I shan't moan, I shan't dread it. I'll say: Christmas? Lovely, what a treat! Because I do like Christmas. I ACCEPT Christmas, I CHOOSE to accept Christmas. HOW I'm looking forward to it! – And that, I hope, will make all the difference in the world.

Once I let the prospect of anything get me down, the Numbers are really able to sink their teeth in and reduce me to a quivering mass of doubt and guilt and self-pity. So I do feel bad myself – often really ill – but that is no excuse, because other people are having to suffer me as that most awful of species, an I'm-Sorry-I-Exist complex on legs. If only the Numbers would see that there is nothing more irritating to other people than someone who is always sorry – but I suppose they will never learn. I have to accept the fact that they will not change, but mercifully, through The Book and the diary and all I have done and thought on this journey, I now possess the means to deal with them.

Christmas is – should be – can be – a lovely time, not a strait-jacket. And so is life and everything in life that I will have to face. If it isn't or cannot be lovely, then it will teach me something out of the bad – strength, wisdom, truth. I choose here and now to accept life and all it may hold for me from now on.

I must remember – I CHOOSE to want to remember – that every sunrise is wonderful, every small bird singing a lesson in joy, every flower blooming an unasked-for gift. Every minute of life is precious. I will not let those Numbers take my moments from me in misery and despair.

It won't be easy, but though I fall again and again, I will I know somehow manage to find myself and pick myself up, and every time I fall, I shall rise stronger. Acknowledging gratefully the love and help I can trust the world to give me in the form (so far) of D.'s steadfastness and caring, Charlotte's wisdom and generosity, Lara's and Neil's affection and ability to matter-of-factly accept an eccentric as a Mum. Vera and Joan, too, who have read copies of the pages in which they are mentioned (since I asked their permission to use their names), and told me they felt honoured to be included in this document.

To me, all of these people sparkle, shine with warmth. My gifts for the turn of the year are the facts that I can feel the glow, that I can see how it lights my days. They say love overcomes all. Maybe in my case, that was what did it. I don't know.

But I am going to say goodbye now. Whatever else happens will only be a playback of the same old story. The Numbers will never give up. But each time I taste the wonder of living, I become more and more determined that, having seen the treasure that was waiting for me at the end of this journey, I will fight not to lose it. It has been worth everything, and I won't give up – I won't give myself up – I won't give any of it up.

So I'll say goodbye. This is the end of my story. Or more importantly, just the beginning.

AFTERWORD: THE AUTHOR TODAY

In the years since the events in this book took place, I have studied and read widely concerning the conditions I appeared to encounter and to suffer from. Depression and 'mania' were perhaps the most obvious to identify, but the anger, shame, guilt and lack of trust and self-worth – an almost textbook description of the effects of childhood rape and sexual abuse – took much longer to recognise.

At the time I wrote the 'Diary', I had dismissed the idea of 'Multiple Personality' because one of the main characteristics of such cases appeared to be the fact that the patient herself (and between 75% and 95% of recorded instances are women) was largely unaware of the existence of secondary personalities. Typically, she suffered from blackouts during the periods when they were active, and had no recollection of what had taken place during that time. Consequently (and this was particularly significant in regard to my own case) the patient had no sense of responsibility for her actions when they had been performed by secondary personalities.

I appeared to retain my awareness all the time and accepted full responsibility for everything I did, though I was often unable to explain my actions or even defend them. Many times I would find myself in the middle of situations where I would all of a sudden 'switch' from being absolutely in control to being blank and bewildered, incapable of making the slightest attempt to cope. Some of these situations were not only foolhardy but put me at actual physical risk, and I long ago accepted it as routine that for some reason I did not know, I might at any time need to be 'rescued' by the goodwill of others.

On many occasions over the years, I have found myself only too aware – bitterly and helplessly aware sometimes – that I could not have manage to keep going except for 'the kindness of strangers', as Blanche Dubois famously expressed it in Tennessee Williams' *A Streetcar Named Desire*. Self-reliance and confidence in my own judgement or even my own sense of reality was almost impossible as a result. But perhaps it was the very fact that in order to survive, desperately needing that kindness, *I generally found it* (though too humiliatingly for a proud spirit to accept with gratitude often), that kept me from blanking out the rest of humanity altogether.

As to the question of whether my situation was brought about by a 'mental illness' that could be clinically charted and identified as some physical imbalance in the brain, or whether it was more dramatic, the result of demonic or other possession, being taken over by negative entities, I do not know. And does it, in the end, really matter? The important thing so far as I am concerned is that with the writing of 'The Book' and Diary in 1987, I was able to put my foot on the road to freedom from my mental prison and take the first step along that road. I have continued working to 'heal' myself ever since and still actively do so for like an addict, I am never going to be 'cured'. One does not put back the broken pieces after an experience of this kind and find there are no joins. One works with the information and wisdom one has been given, enlarging one's horizons all the time so that one can transcend and become greater than the sum of one's parts.

The situation was actually far more complicated than I had thought. There were more personalities which were not so evident as the Numbers – the murderous angry face that showed itself during my outbursts of fury and the 'hate attack' was one. And much later – five years later, actually, when I was ready to become aware of my psychic potential – a calming, wise presence which is also apparently yet another characteristic of many recorded 'Multiple Personality' cases revealed itself. This ISH (Inner Spiritual Helper) encouraged me to find strength, stability and peace within myself.

And whether this presence was actually my own Higher Self or some form of alternative psychiatric persona, a Spirit Guide or simply my own creation – another 'mad' delusion – is again, to me, irrelevant. It is there, it is very real to me and with its wisdom and light, guides my steps and brightens my life. The gifts it brings are entirely positive, enlightening and transforming.

During the last ten years or so, working as a psychic counsellor in London, the South of England and the Midlands, I have been able to see for myself the courage and fortitude – as well as the immense spiritual potential - of hundreds of so-called 'ordinary' people who have needed to undertake similar mental journeys to 'heal' themselves. My books about my work have brought me letters from all parts of the world, Australia, Europe and America as well as the British Isles. Many of the people who have consulted me have had the same problems I encountered myself: difficulty in forming or maintaining relationships, feeling unable to trust or love; desperate for reassurances of their own worth, that they would be safe and secure in the future, or that their fear and pain would be taken away.

Some have been trapped in 'double bind' situations – which, while typical of families prone to schizophrenia, may develop in non-schizophrenic families and can be passed down through mother to daughter (again women are most often the victims) for years unless the syndrome is broken. Some are afraid they are going mad because their realities do not seem to be the same as other people's.

Because of the journey I made myself, I am hopefully able to identify their situations to some degree and perhaps assist them, even if only with encouragement and acknowledgement of their effort and their progress. Ultimately, we all have to make our journey on our own, find our own reality and achieve our own wholeness. It may help though, simply to know that others have passed along this road, others have been this way before you – and survived.

APPENDIX : 'THE DOUBLE BIND'
(From the original Chapter 1 of Tanya's Book)

'...The wrist-cutting (at age twenty-three) resulted in my first spell in a mental hospital. I recovered my equilibrium quite quickly but was told nothing helpful about why I should have been unable to cope to the extent that I felt I wanted to die. I did, however, continue to see a Psychiatric Social Worker for about eighteen months and she explained – largely, I think, because I asked probing questions – about the basics of Freudian thinking and also something that seemed to me to be the answer to everything.

'There have been many answers to everything in the course of my mental ups and downs. Every one gives new hope. It becomes glaringly obvious what has been wrong with me all the time. It offers the final solution to my problems. Until the next time the enemy strikes.

'The theory my Social Worker friend explained to me was that of the 'double-bind' situation, which I will outline as I understood it. If anyone reads this and thinks as I did that it sounds like the answer to everything, I am sure a doctor or psychiatrist will be happy to explain further (or correctly, if I get it slightly wrong).

'There are four components to this sort of situation, which can attach itself to any action at all. I will use the action of sweeping the floor. The components are:

1. You *must* sweep the floor.
2. You *must* not (or *cannot*) sweep the floor.

3. You are *unaware* of the conflict set up by these opposing directives.
4. There is *no escape*.

'I told a friend about the 'double-bind' a few weeks ago. She has had problems with depression in the past but has successfully overcome them with the help of her loving family and is blessedly happy and sane, living a normal, fulfilling life.

'She thought about what I had said then made the comment that if all four components of the situation were present, she couldn't see what anybody could do to break the deadlock.

' "What *do* you do?" she asked....'

More books by Dilys Gater:

CELTIC WISE WOMAN
UNDERSTANDING SECOND SIGHT
IN AND OUT THE WINDOWS
COME SHINING THROUGH: Travelling Hopefully
Etc

Also available in Large Print

A PSYCHIC'S CASEBOOK
PAST LIVES: Case Histories of Previous Existence
Etc

Ask at your local library